ISBN 978-0-266-90396-3
PIBN 10907366

Records of Fort St George

Madras (Presidency) Record Office

DIARY

AND

CONSULTATION BOOK

OF

1704

WITH AN INTRODUCTION

BY

A. V. VENKATARAMA AYYAR, M.A., L.T.

Curator, Madras Record Office

MADRAS
PRINTED BY THE SUPERINTENDENT, GOVERNMENT PRESS

1928

INTRODUCTION

In the present volume are printed the proceedings of the President and Council of Fort St. George for the year 1704, comprised in the thirty-third volume of the manuscript series "Diary and Consultation Books". The manuscript volume has been mended in this office. We are deeply indebted to the India Office who had the kindness to fill in the many gaps and *lacunæ* therein.

1704 was the sixth year of the famous governorship of Thomas Pitt, well-known as the Great President. The volume before us contains several interesting items of information and a few are noted below :—

Doctor Edward Bulkley claimed a palanquin allowance to look after the sick and married soldiers wandering up and down the Black Town, alleging that the same was allowed in other parts of India and considering the reasonableness of the request, he was given a sum of four pagodas per mensem towards the same (page 2).

Daud Khan, the then Nawab of the Carnatic, was given a present of liquors to the value of about thirty pagodas, evidently to keep him in good humour (page 3).

There was a general complaint of abuses in the measuring of grain upon which the Governor got a *markāl* struck according to the custom of England and ordered that all grain in future was to be bought and sold according to the new measure (pages 3 and 12).

Father Michael applied to the Governor for leave to go to Pondicherry, as he had been summoned thither by one who called himself the patriarch of Antioch, the chief priest of the Roman Church. The Governor in Council strongly resented this interference and declared in emphatic terms that he would not allow the patriarch to exercise any authority over the priests that lived under him and enjoined Father Michael not to stir outside the town and even asked officers to see that he did not go outside the gates of Fort St. George (page 6).

We hear of cases of reward and punishment offered to the Company's servants : for example, Ensign Harris who had often been reprimanded for drinking to excess and consequent neglect of duty was, however, later on permitted, provided he mended his ways, to serve as a serjeant in consideration of the fact that he was a family man with his wife and children to maintain (page 9). Coniers of the Gun Room crew, whose pay was stopped on account of drink and neglect of duty, was however paid back his arrears in testimony of his reformation (page 12). Raworth, a sober and diligent man, who promised to be a useful and profitable servant of the Company, was raised from the position of merchant to a Councillor in the vacancy caused by the death of Mr. Ellis (page 19).

Peter de Pometa to whom an arrack lease was given was strictly enjoined not to put anything into the arrack, more especially *datura*, that was destructive to the health of the people (page 23).

Governor Pitt strongly resented the action of the Faujdar at San Thome in imprisoning some of the Company's servants and replied to him in strong and dignified terms, still ringing in our ears : " We would have you to know we are of a Nation whose Sovereign as great and powerful, able to protect his subjects in their just rights over all the world, and revenge whatever injustices should be done them, of which there will be speedy instances given. I am not a little surprised at your saucy expressions, as well as actions in imprisoning my inhabitants, when you know I can fetch you hither and correct you for both . . . " (page 22).

The Governor in Council appointed a Committee of four to enquire into a complaint made by the widow of one Wollacca Chetty against injustices done to her by one Chinandee Chetty and report the result to the Governor in Council with the least possible delay (page 55).

The Portuguese Roman Catholics of Madras petitioned the President and Governor of the Council of Fort St. George that their wills and testaments should, as has been the case for the previous sixty-two years, be approved by the Capuchin Fathers and not at the Court of the Honourable Company, as they had been ordered recently, and requested that they should be judged according to the customs of the Portuguese Nation. They also complained that the new procedure would entail greater cost (page 65).

Yegmore (Egmore), Persiawaeke (Purasawakum) and Tandore (Tondiarpet), the three new towns were leased to Kittee Narrain for seven years for thirteen hundred pagodas per annum (page 67).

On the death intestate of a Portuguese Captain Francisco de Saa during his voyage to Batavia, it was ordered that an inventory should be made of all money, goods, books and papers in his hands at the time of his death and that after paying all his debts according to the Portuguese law, a moiety should go to his widow and the remainder was to be in the Company's possession until demanded by his relatives, in Europe, who had a right thereto (page 75).

House-keeper Empson of Fort St. George though he was transferred on promotion to Fort St. David as a mark of favour to be Second in Council there preferred to resign his place, inasmuch as it was inconvenient as he had settled himself with his large family as a house-keeper in Fort St. George for 11 years and had lived there 18 years. He wanted that the whole affair should be recorded in the Consultation Book so that his Honourable Masters in England might peruse the same (page 75).

A Moor snatched away a candle of a young Portuguese woman as she was walking in procession and from this petty incident a quarrel soon broke out between the two nations, the Portuguese and the Moors, and the Governor of the Portuguese Nation sought the help of the Company's Governor (page 83).

On receipt of a letter from a Gentu contained in a sealed cover dropped in the Company's gardens complaining against the frauds committed by the storekeepers, rental-general, scavengers and conicoplyes of the Company, a notice was put up in all languages, as the complaint did not contain particulars, inviting the person concerned to appear before the Governor and prove the allegations on promise of a reward of fifty pagodas, etc. (page 98).

The Governor in Council thought it advisable to take some notice of the son of Yassama Naigue (Yachama Nayak) then remaining at Trivlecane (Triplicane) by giving him a small present, as he was in a considerable post and governed a country from which many goods were imported to Madras (page 104).

MADRAS RECORD OFFICE,
EGMORE,
Dated 30th March 1928.

A. V. VENKATARAMA AYYAR,
Curator.

RECORDS OF FORT ST. GEORGE

DIARY AND CONSULTATION BOOK

OF

1704 ·

(VOLUME No. 33)

[*From December 29, 1703, to December 22, 1704.*]

——*RECORDS OF FORT ST. GEORGE, 170¾*——

**The Consultation and Diary Book of Thomas Pitt Esqr: President·
& Govr: &cᵃ: Councill their Proceedings and Transactions in·
the Affairs of the Rt: Honᵇˡᵉ: English East India Company in
the Presidency of the Coast of Choromandell &cᵃ: Begun the
29th December 1703.**

AT A CONSULTATION

[DECEM-
BER 1703]

Present

THOMAS PITT ESQ., PRESIDENT AND GOVERNᴿ.
WILLIAM FRASER.   THOMAS MARSHALL.
THOMAS WRIGHT.   JOHN MEVERELL.·

WEDNES-
DAY 29ᵀᴴ.
(1703)

Ordered that the Warehousekeeper and Mʳ. Fraser in presence of the Two
Assay Masters do open the Chests of Gold No. A and B now come upon the
Tavestock, and weigh it and deliver it to the Mint Master.

Ordered that all Stores in the Garrison in Charge of the Warehousekeeper be
delivered to Mᶠ. Fraser.

Ordered that the Warehousekeeper Mʳ. Fraser Load forty-five Tons of Redwood as the Kentilage of Ship Tarestock also Load sixty Tons more on said Ship
to send to Bengal for the Kentilage of their Ships, and accordingly he is order'd
to buy the same.

Agreed that One Thousand Pagodas be pay'd Mr. John Meverell Paymaster
for defraying Charges Garrison.

THOMAS PITT.
WILLIAM FRASER.
THOMAS WRIGHT.
THOMˢ: MARSHALL.
JOHN MEVERELL.

Received per patamar a Generall Letter from Mʳ. Tillard at Metchlepatam.
Ship Alla Bux Bauker Beague Noquedah arrived in this road from Ceilone.

JANUARY
8ᴰ.

ATT A CONSULTATION

Present

TH[OMAS PITT ESQ.ᴿ.] PRESIDENT & [GOVᴿ.] ·
[*Lacuna*]   WILLIAM FRASER.
THOMAS WRIGHT.   THOMAS [MARSHALL].
JOHN MEVERE[LL].

TUESDAY
4ᵀᴴ.

Mʳ. William Fraser &cᵃ. delivers in their report of the condition of the Cloth
receiv'd by Ship Tavestock as entered after this Consultation.

-----*FORT ST. GEORGE, JANUARY 1704*-----

M^r. William Fraser &c^a. delivers in their report of the weighing of two Chests of Gold received ℔ ship Tavestock which were found to be wanting oz. 6 8 ^{d. wt.} the report to be sent home by the first ship.

Ordered that M^r. Thomas Wright, M^r. John Meverell, M^r. Gulston Addison and M^r. Robert Raworth be Justices at the Choultry.

Agreed that Five Hundred Pagodas be advanc'd M^r. Thomas Marshall Paymaster for defraying Charges Garrison.

The Governour and Council having on the 18th. of last month appointed severall Persons in their Employes in the United Companys Service, who were this day sent for and acquainted, who according to their orders were desired to write to their Freinds in England to give the usuall Securitys.

Ordered that Messrs. Fraser, Marshall & Meverell take an Inventory of the dead stock of this Place, and make their remarks what condition everything is in, to be sent to the Company by the Colchester.

Doct^r. Edward Bulkley Complaining that y^e. marryed men who are souldiers liveing stragling up and down the Black Town makes it impossible for him to looke after them in their sickness, without being at the Charge of a Pallankeen, and often urgeing that the same is allowed in all other parts of India which we believe to be so, so considering the reasonableness of his request have agreed that he be allowed Four Pagodas p^r. mensem towards the charge thereof to be pay'd by the Paymaster.

M^r. Affleck having made some overtures for the boxes of silver Plate sent on the Tavestock likewise offered to sell the Company 450 Baggs of Salt Petre. Tis ordered that M^r. Fraser discourse him about the same and report it to the Govern^r. & Council.

> THOMAS PITT.
> WILL: FRASER.
> THOMAS MARSHALL.
> JOHN MEVERELL.

THE HON^{ble}: THOMAS PITT Esqr.
  PRESIDENT AND GOVERNOUR OF FORT
    S^T. GEORGE &c^a. COUNCIL.

In persuance of an order of Council of the 24th. Instant we view'd the eleven Bales received p^r. Ship Tavestock suspected to be damaged, but find the damage to be so very little that we think with submission it's for our Honble. Masters' Interest not to deliver any of them to the Captain, We are

Hon^r. Sir^r.
Your most humble servants, etc.

FORT S^T. GEORGE,
  29 DEC^R. 170¾.

7TH. Ship Jakernacolo sail'd southward.

8. Received ℔ Pattamars two Generalls from the Deputy Governour and Council of Fort S^t. David dated 3^d. or 4th. Ins^t.

9. Ketch Queen Anne arrived this road from Vizagapatam by whom received a Generall Letter from the Chief and Council there dated 29th Instant advising the arrivall there of Ship Dutchess having lost her Passage from Atcheen to Bengall, put in there for refreshments being a very sickly ship.

—— FORT ST. GEORGE, JANUARY 1704 ——

AT A CONSULTATION

Present

THOMAS PITT ESQR. PRESIDENT & GOVERNR.
[*Lacuna*] WILLIAM FRASER.
THOMAS WRIGHT. THOMAS MARSHALL.
JOHN MEVERELL.

Mr. Matthew Empson late Sea Customer reads his Sea Custom Accounts for the months of November and Decemr Vizt

Account Custome ... ... Pa. 1,133 : 21 : 15
Freight ⅌ Mary Bowyear ... .. 11 : 19 : 14

Pag. 1,145 : 4 : 29

and pays into the Honble. United Companys Cash the sum of eleven hundred forty-five Pagodas four fanams and twenty-nine cash.

Mr. William Warr Register payes into the Rt Honble. United Companys Cash the sume of sixteen Pagodas eight fanams for Account fees of the Court of Admiralty.

Ordered that Mr William Fraser Warehousekeeper payes the Vizagapatam Bill of Exchange received yesterday for Three thousand Rupees; in Madrass Rupees being equall in value to the Rupees of that Country.

Agreed that One Thousand Pagodas be payd Mr. Thomas Marshall Paymaster for defraying Charges Garrison.

Thomas Pitt Esqr President reads his Account of the Rt Honble. United Companys Cash for the month of December Ballance Pagods. 521.

Ordered that the Warehousekeeper do inquire if any Persons will buy the broad cloth come on the Tavestock by private Contract, or else will be sold by Outcry.

Generall Letter from the Deputy Governour and Council of Fort St. David dated 3d. Instant now read.

Agreed that a Present of Liquors to the Amount of about Thirty Pagodas, be provided and sent Nabob Daud Cawn.

There having been a Generall Complaint of Great abuses in measuring of Grain, upon which the Governour made a Mercall to strike according to the Custom of England; which was this day produc'd before the Council and found that when it was struck it held a full mercall of the Country, on which 'tis Agreed that Twelve more be made, and all other measures accordingly, after which all Grain to be bought and sold by the same.

It haveing been an old Custom hitherto for the Oylemen of this Place to find oxen to fetch Chinam for wch it has been usuall to pay them Four Pagodas ⅌ Parrah which was so little that it would not near pay for the meat of the Ox, and the man for which reason they kept but few, which made it very tedious in building for want of Chunam, besides we have often and frequent clamours from the Inhabitants by reason of scarcity of the same upon which we have thought it necessary to advance the ox-hire to six Doodas a Parrah, and order that the Paymaster advance One Hundred Pagodas to the Oylemen to buy them more oxen, and to deduct it out of their hire.

Mr. Fraser Reports that he has discoursed Mr. Affleck about the silver, who will give no more then Fiveteen and three quarters Dollars for Ten Pagodas, which is ordered to be deliver'd him, in regard he designs it for China, which will be an advantage not only to the Company in their Custom but likewise an encouragement to the Trade of the Place. Mr. Fraser also reports that Mr. Affleck will not sell his Salt Petre under 14½ Pagods. ⅌ Candy, upon which we acquainted we could give no answer thereto till after the arrival of the Colchester.

―――― *FORT ST. GEORGE, JANUARY 1704* ――――

We having no Arrac in store and daily fearing the troubles from the Country, when we shall more particularly have occasion for the same. Tis ordered that the Steward buys twelve Leakers of Battavia Arrac there being so offered to sale at reasonable rates.

> THO: PITT.
> WILL: FRASER.
> THO: WRIGHT.
> THOM⁸. MARSHALL.
> JOHN MEVERELL.

11ᵗ.   Dispatch'd ℔ Pattamars Two Generall Letters to the Deputy Governour and Council of Fort Sᵗ. David Vizᵗ. one for the United Trade, the other for the seperate both dated 10ᵗʰ. Instant.

12ᵀᴴ.   Received ℔ Pattamar a Generall Letter from Mʳ. Faucett &cᵃ. Council at Metchlepatam dated 4ᵗʰ. Instant; as also a Letter from the Governour and Council of Pollicat datᵈ. yᵗ. day.

―――――

AT A CONSULTATION

Present

THOMAS PITT ESQ². PRESIDENT AND GOVERNOUR.
THURSDAY
13ᵀᴴ.   THOMAS WRIGHT.   WILLIAM FRASER.
JOHN MEVERELL.   THOMAS MARSHALL.

Thomas Pitt Esqʳ. as Mintmaster reads his Mint Account for the month of December last, and pays into the Rᵗ. Honᵇˡᵉ. United Companys Cash the sum of One Hundred and eight Pagodas thirty one fanam forty Cash for Accoᵗ. Custom Gold coined in the mint.

There being severall things lying in the Sea Gate Godown the Proprietors of which are unknown; Ordered that Mʳ. Thomas Wright Sea Customer puts up a notice on the Sea Gate giving notice of the same, and if no owner thereof appears within a month, then to be sold at Outcry, and the produce thereof paid into the Compʸˢ. Cash.

Mʳ. Joseph Hiller Provissionall Storekeeper reads his Storekeeper's Account for the months of Decembʳ. and November last.

Ordered that Domingo Leam Topaz be Entertainᵈ. Souldier in this Garrison.

This day severall Casts were before us concerning reimbursing Serapan what he lay'd out by their consent and approbation when Doud Cawn was here for which he has their obligation under their Hands, for the reimbursing of which they propose no other then when last before us as ℔ Consultation 24ᵗʰ past month Tis resolved that Serapan sues them in the Court for the Amount he disburs'd wᵗʰ. the Interest.

> THO: PITT.
> WILL: FRASER.
> THO: WRIGHT.
> THOM⁸. MARSHALL.
> JOHN MEVERELL.

Ship Maddapollam Noquedah Laulusaunder arrived in this road from Arrackan.

Dispatch'd ℔ Pattamar a Generall Letter to the Deputy Governour and Council at Pollicat dated this day.

14.   Last night the Governour received newes by a Portuguez Letter from Pondicherry that the Two French Ships were returned with an English prize called the Canturbury belonging to the New East India Coʸ. having mett her

——FORT ST. GEORGE, JANUARY 1704——

and M^r. Dolben in the Chamber's Frigat in the streights of Malacca, which was this day confirm'd to us by a Letter from Pondicherry copy of which as follows, Viz^t.

The two French Vessells mett the Chambers Friggat and another of the new Company's called the Canterbury of more than 300 Tons, commanded by Capt. Kingsford, came from England and bound to Surat. The 19th. December near the Island Sambelàm in the streights of Malacca at night gave each other broad sides, The Chambers Friggat had main ar disabled, which he got repair'd in the night next morning she fought again during 4 hours against the lesser French Ship, after which he made all the sail he [could] to banck of Parsàla the Maurepas fought again the Canterbury, which he took immediately, Monseiur de Fontenay was sent against the Chamber's Friggat who seem'd the least, but proved the biggest and best man. We hear f^rom those we have taken that M^r. Dolben gave 50 Guineys to each man, and a promise to each that should be wounded to provide for them, to the end they sho^d. behave themselves well.

Ship Colchester Capt. Alexander Reid Commander arrived in this road from Bengall, by whom received a Generall Letter from the President and Council there dated 15th. December.   15.

From M^r. William Tillard at Metchlepatam dated the 10th Instant.

From M^r. Stephen Fremen &c^a. Councill there dated 11th. Ditto, inclosing an Inventory of the Dead Stock of both Factorys.

M^r. Frewen, &c.^a R^t. Honble. Company's servants came on this Ship, delivering up the charge of both our Factorys of Metchlepatam and Madapollam to M^r. Tillard with the dead stock of the old Company.

AT A CONSULTATION

Present

THOMAS PITT ESQ^R. PRESIDENT & GOVERNOUR.
     FRANCIS ELLIS.   WILLIAM FRASER.
     THOMAS WRIGHT.   THOMAS MARSHALL.
         JOHN MEVERELL.

         MONDAY 17TH.

Agreed that the following Companys servants be sent to Fort S^t. David Viz^t.

    M^R. LANDON MINISTER.
    M^R. RICHARD HARRISON.
    M^R. JAMES LYDE.
    M^R. NATHANIEL BABROW.
    M^R. MATTHEW WELD.
    M^R. JOHN S_cARLET.
    M^R. VILLERS HAVENINGHAM.
    M^R. WILLIAM DIXON.

There being offered about Five hundred Candy of Redwood to sale at two and a quarter Pagodas ℔ Candy. Tis orderd the Warehousekeeper buys the same, it being the Company's order to supply Bengall and the West Coast with that commodity as opportunitys offer.

There being considerable quantitys of stores as Rice, Wheat &c^a. brought from Bengall on the Colchester Tis ordered that M^r. Fraser receives them from M^r. Wright for Account of the United Company, which are to be valued according to the prizes Currant of this Place.

                     THO. PITT.
                     WILL : FRASER.
                     THO : WRIGHT.
                     THOM^s. MARSHALL.
                     JOHN MEVERELL.

18TH.

The Governour this day received copy of a Letter from Capt. Kingsford to the Deputy Governour of Fort St. David adviseing of his being taken by the French Ships, and that he and 54 Englishmen were at Pondicherry.

Dispatch'd ℗ Pattamars a Generall Letter to M^r. William Tillard at Mechlepatam dated this day.

Dispatch'd Pattamars a Letter to the Generall at Council at Surat dated yesterday.

Ship Prince Charles belonging to the Royall Danish arrived in this Road from Bengall by whom received a Generall Letter from the President and Councill there dated 31st. past month.

AT A CONSULTATION

SATURDAY
22º.

Present

THOMAS PITT ESQ^R. PRESIDENT & GOVERNOUR.
THOMAS WRIGHT.   WILLIAM FRASER.
JOHN MEVERELL.   THOMAS MARSHALL.

Ordered that the Warehousekeeper sells the United Company's Lead at 8 Pag. ℗ Candy; and ordinary Broad cloth at 17 Pag^s. ℗ Peice.

Padre Michael having applyed himself to the Govr. for leave to go to Pondicherry, for that he that calls him the Patriarch of Antioch had summoned him thither and he feared that if he did not goe 'twould tend to his ruin the Governour deferred giving him leave till he had consulted his Council, which was this day summoned and Padre Michael sent for, who earnestly insisted for leave to go who was ask't by the Governour whether the Patriarch sent for him as Chief Priest of this Romish Church or on any other Account, he answered that 'twas as he was Chief Priest; to which 'twas replyed that we could allow of no Persons to have any Authority over the Priests of this Place, so as to send for them away, or return them or any others at their pleasure, and supposing the abbot to have heard in this matter we sent for him, who jesuitically evaded, and denyed that he knew anything of the matter, whom likewise we acquainted with our resolution that the Patriarch, nor none else should exercise any power over the Priests that lives under our Government, so dismis them both, strictly enjoining Padre Michael not to stir out of the Town, besides that Orders should be given the officers not to permitt him to go without the Gates.

The Brickmakers being 500 Pagodas in Debt still pressed for some more money for that they are preparing to make great quantitys of bricks this season the materialls for which being visible so that the Company can't suffer by advancing 3 or 400 Pag. more, 'tis agreed that the Paymaster does the same.

The Third's Lodgings being very much out of repair which M^r. William Fraser desires to live in, 'tis ordered the Paymaster repairs the same.

M^r. Fraser having acquainted us before that M^r. Affleck would not sell his Petre under 14½ Pag^s. ℗ Candy, and we hearing from Bengall by the Colchester that both the old and new Company, more particularly the former had provided a great quantity thereof, which must be disposed of to the Council for the United Trade, so that 'tis resolved we desist from buying M^r. Affleck's.

THO: PITT.
WILL: FRASER.
THO: WRIGHT.
THOM^s. MARSHALL.
JOHN MEVERELL.

——— *FORT ST. GEORGE, JANUARY 1704* ———

At a Consultation

Present

Thomas Pitt Esqʳ., President and Governʳ.　　　Monday
Thomas Wright.　　William Fraser,　　　　　　24ᵗʰ.
John Meverell.　　Thomas Marshall.

Generall Letter from the Deputy Governour and Council of Fort Sᵗ. David dated the 20ᵗʰ. Instant now read.

Padre Michael Ange Chief Padre of the Portuguez Church delivered in a Petition yesterday to the Governour and Council for leave to go to Pondicherry, which was now read and an answer given thereto, as Entered after this Consultation.

In Chest Nº. 109 containing severall Private person's silver, which was all delivered as Directed except Charles Boon who is in Bengall, which is ordered to be sent him by the Tavestock and Mʳ. Stone's is delivered to the President at the request of Mʳ. Roberts.

> Tho : Pitt.
> Will: Fraser.
> Tho : Wright.
> Thomˢ. Marshall.
> John Meverell.

Illustrissimo Domino Gubernatori,
　　Nobilibus que arcis Sancti Georgy
　　　Consubbus.
　　　Illustrissimi Domini.

Per multum Importat mihi pergere in Pondicherry, ad meas superiores a quibus vocatus sum, qua propter hepi humillime et Instantissime Licentiam petii Dominationibus vestris ad illuc eundum, et nodie iterum atque candum Instantius rogo, sperans quod nuhi hanc concedere non Dedignetur, Datum in Arce Sᵗ. Georgij Die 23ᵈ. January 1703.

> T: Michael Angelus.

Reverendo in Deo Patri Michaelo Angelo.

Vestra hesterno die data recepie bamus, et quom pridie responsum dedimus satisfacturum existimebamus, utpote Domino Gubernatori in Concilio vobis suscitantianum Patriarchœ Mandato rium vos ad Pondicherry ordinavit veluti hujus Ecclesiœ Primatem vel alio existente negotio, responsam retulisti te veluti sacredotem appulsurum, qua propter sententiam ferebamus nos nulli concessuras potestatem veloum sacerdotibus vel alij in nostris versantibus mænies rem habende quorsum ut vestro obstruaremus decissni ordnavmus ut intra mœni anglicania Arcis corrceris constituentes si egredires in hanc Ecclesiam nunquam reversurum quœ omnia his germantur, Datis sub manibus nostris in Arce sᵗⁱ. Georg Decimo quarto Die 1703/4.

> Thoms. Pitt.
> William Fraser.
> Thos. Wright.
> Thos. Marshall.
> John. Meverell

—— FORT ST GEORGE, JANUARY 1704 ——

At a Consultation

Present

[Th]urs-
day 27ᴵᴴ.

Thomas Pitt Esqʳ. President and Governᵣ.
WILLIAM FRASER.
Thomas Wright. Thomas Marshall.
John Meverell.

Mʳ. Richard Hunt late Provissionall Land Customer reads his Land Custom Account for the month of December and payes into the Rᵗ. Honᵇˡᵉ. United Companys Cash the sume of Two hundred fifty five Pagodas twentysix fanams and thirty Cash.

Ordered that one Thousand Pagodas be paid Mʳ. Thomas Marshall Paymaster for defraying Charges Garrison, and that One Thousand Pagodas more be advanced him towards building the Black Town Wall and works.

Mʳ. William Fraser Warehousekeeper payes into the Rᵗ. Honᵇˡᵉ. United Companys Cash the sume of two Thousand Pagodas on Account silver sold.

Generall Letter to the Rᵗ. Honᵇˡᵉ. Mannagers to Par 75 now read and approved.

Mʳ. Thomas Wright Warehousekeeper reads his Account what Goods received ⅌ Ship Tavestock for the United Account, and delivers them to Mʳ. William Fraser who is Warehousekeeper for the United Trade.

Ordered that George Tompson be discharged the Gunroome Crew in this Garrison.

All Cloth being cheapest of late to the Southward 'Tis agreed that we write to the Deputy Governʳ. and Council of Fort Sᵗ. David and remitt them, the List of Goods the Mannagers for the United Trade have ordered to be bought, with their particular direction about investments, and upon receipt of which to summon the Merchants and acquaint therewith and if any body will undertake for those sorts of Goods for them as they bring them in : That then they make musters, and send them with all expedition with the prices thereof.

Tho. Pitt.
Will. Fraser.
Tho. Wright.
Thomᵀ. Marshall.
John Meverell.

Dispatchd ⅌ Pattamar a Generall Letter to the Deputy Governour and Council of Fort Sᵗ. David for Trade dated this day.

Received ⅌ Pattamars a Generall Letter from William Tillard Chief for the new Companys affairs at Metchlepatam dated 20ᵗʰ: Instant with a box of papers Directed to the Directors for the New Company's affairs and a Pacqᵗ: for the Honᵇˡᵉ. Managers.

At a Consultation

Present

[Febru-
ary] 3ᴰ.

Thomas Pitt Esqʳ. President & Governour.
WILLIAM FRASER. Thomas Marshall.
Thomas Wright. John Meverell.

Thomas Pitt Esqʳ. President reads his Account of the Rᵗ. Honᵇˡᵉ. United Companys Cash for the month of January last Ballance Pagᵃ. 546 : 34 : 1 :

Thomas Pitt Esqʳ: as Mintmaster payes into the Rᵗ. Honᵇˡᵉ. United Company's Cash the sume of Twenty three Thousand Pagodᵃ. for Gold coined in the **Mint** received ⅌ Ship Tavestock.

——*FORT ST. GEORGE, FEBRUARY 1704*——

Ordered that Thomas Lecroy be Entertained a Sould^r. in this Garrison.

The Gentlemen who were ordered for Fort S^t. David the 17th. past month were now sent for, and ordered to get ready to go on Satturday next.

Ordered that the Warehousekeeper do load on Ketch Queen Ann the following Goods and Stores Viz^t.

Bales.

8. Broad cloth Ordinary red.
8. Ditto Green.
3. Aurora.
1. Scarlet.

One brass Morter with Carriage :—
    100 Finelock Musekets, 50 with Baggonetts.
    10 Pair Pistolls,
    100 Amunition Swords.
10,000 Musquet Flints.
    5 Barrell's English Powder 1 of which Pistoll.

£
100,000 Europe match.
    500 Saker shott.
    100 Faulken Ditto.
    1 Searcher.
    500 Granadoe shells.

Generall Letter from Mr. William Tillard at Metchlepatam dated the 20th past month now read.

Mr. John Meverell Late Paymaster reads his Paymaster's Account for the month of December last, Viz^t.

Charges Garrison	...	...	...	...	Pag. 1,239 : 22 :
Charges Cattle	...	...	...	...	60: 20:
Silk Wormes	...	...	...	...	17 : 23 :
Black Stone	...	...	...	...	15:
Charges Generall	...	...	...	...	418 : 23 :
Charges Extraordinary	...	...	...		58: 21:
Charges Dyet	...	...	...	...	501 : 1 :
Fortifications and repairs	...	...	...		283 : 18 :

Pags. 2,594 : 20 :

and Payes into the Rt. Honble. United Company's cash the summe of One Hundred eighty six Pag^s. eight fanams as the Ballance of his Paymaster's Account.

Agreed that One Thousand Pagod^s. be paid Mr. Thomas Marshall Paymaster for defraying Charges Garrison.

Ordered that Robert Hunt at his request be discharged from further service in this garrison.

Ensign Harris who has often been found drunk in so much that he has been uncapable of doing his duty, for which he has been frequently reprehended but finding it to no purpose he was this day broak; but in regard he has a Wife and severall Children we have permitted him to serve as Serjeant, but that no longer than he abstains from drinking to excess.

THO. PITT.
WILLIAM FRASER.
THO. WRIGHT.
THOM^s. MARSHALL.
JOHN MEVERELL.

—FORT ST. GEORGE, FEBRUARY 1704—

5.   Capᵗ. Kingsford late Comander of Ship Canturbury which the French took her arrived here this morning overlands from Pondicherry.

     Dispatchᵈ. ⅌ Pattamars a Generall Letter to the Dy. Governour and Councill of Fort St. David for the separate Affairs dated this day.

6.   Twenty of Ship Canturbury's men arrived in town from Pondicherry.

7.   Queen Anne Ketch sailed out of this road for Fort St. David upon which went the Factors and writers ordered for that place.

8.   Dispatched ⅌ Pattamar a Generall Letter to the Deputy Governour and Councill of Fort St. David for the United Trade.

9.   Sloop Ulumbane arrived in this road from Trincombar.

10.   Between 3 and 4 this morning Ship Tavestock fired two Guns to give notice two ships were coming into the road, who were suspected to be French but proved to be the Stretham Capᵗ. Flint Comander from Batavia, and the Malborough separate Stock Ship Capᵗ. Minter Commander from Emoy in China.

AT A CONSULTATION

Present

THOMAS PITT ESQʳ. PRESIDENT & GOVERNOUR.

FRYDAY.   WILLIAM FRASER.   THOMAS WRIGHT.
11.   THOMAS MARSHALL.   JOHN MEVERELL.

   Ponagette Narso &cᵃ., Tobacco and Beetle farmers pays into the Rᵗ. Honᵇˡᵉ: United Companys Cash the sume of seven Hundred Pagodas on that Account.

   Gruapa &cᵃ: Arrac Farmers payes into the Rᵗ. Honᵇˡᵉ. United Companys Cash the sume of Three hundred and fifty Pagodˢ. on that Account.

   Messʳˢ. Fraser, Marshall, and Meverell, delivers in yᵉ. Account remaines of the Dead Stock in this Place as ordered ⅌ Consultation the 4th January last.

   Mʳ. John Meverell Paymaster reads his Accounts of money received from the Inhabitants Account Black Town Wall, and payes One Hundred Pagodas as the Ballance of that Account, as also reads his Accoᵗ. disbursements of the Black Town Wall and payes one hundred and seven Pagˢ. thirty fanams and forty four Cash as the Ballance of that Account.

   Ordered that Domingo de Roz and Antonio Fereiro Cofferees be Entertaind souldiers in this Garrison.

   Thomas Pitt Esqʳ. as Mintmaster payes into the Rᵗ. Honᵇˡᵉ. United Companys Cash the sume of thirty two thousand six hundred forty five Pagodas as the Ballance of Gold received ⅌ Ship Tavestock coined in the Mint.

   Capᵗ. Kingsford having adrest himself to Governour concerning a report his men had given out of their ill usage and his misbehaving himself at the time he engaged with the French, at which he seem'd much concerned it tending to the ruin of his reputation, so desired that he and his officers might be heard face to face before the Governour and Councill which was this day done, when upon hearing what his officers had to say, and the Captain's answere thereto and the many questions that was ask't both partys we found that the men had reason to complain of their hard usage for want of Provissions whilst in China, but for any thing of misbehaving himself whilst engaged with the enemy, we believe that part more malice than truth.

   Mr. Brewster, Mr. Daniel, &c. Supra Cargoes of Ship Strutham with their Commander complained to us, against Mr. Richard Grimes that was now their Cheif Mate of insufferable Abuses and Affronts they had receiv'd from him, who being sent for to answer the same was now before us, who could not deny what they charg'd him with, which was threatning them all, that he would slitt their

—————*FORT ST. GEORGE, FEBRUARY 1704*—————

noses, and cutt their throats, and a great deal of approbrious language, of which he confess'd himself guilty, but would have excus'd it as being drunk, besides the Commander and Supra Cargoes charg'd him with intollerable debauchery of all sorts, and with it gave it as their Opinions that it was not safe for the Comps. Estate, nor for the security of the Shipp that he should longer continue in her, and wee being all of us of the same opinion 'twas agree'd that he should be discharg'd, and the Cheif Mate of the Canterbury shipt in his room, After the Supra Cargoes inform'd us that Mr. Grimes had taken up two Hundred Pounds at Bottomary for which Captain Moyers was bound, which money was demanded of Mr. Grimes or that he would give security to indemnifie the Widdow, unto which he answer'd that he had spent part of it, and some was on board the Ship. Order'd that Captain Flint should give him no acknowledgment for his wages, nor suffer any thing of his to be taken out of the Ship till he had given satisfaction in this matter.

> Thomas Pitt.
> William Fraser.
> Thom. Marshall.
> John Meverell.

Receiv'd pr. Pattamarrs Two Pacquets from the Deputy Govr. and Councill of Fort St. David, one for the United Trade the other for the seperate. **12.**

Sloop Ganjees arriv'd in this road from Fort St. David. **13.**

This evening about Four Ship Colchester fir'd a Gun and spread her Colours to signifie she was full.

Att a Consultation

Present

Thomas Pitt Esq̄ᴿ. President and Governᴿ.
William Fraser.   Thomas Wright.
Thomas Marshall ·   John Meverell.

Tuesday 15th.

Agreed that One Thousand Pagodas be pay'd Mr. Thomas Marshall Paymaster for defraying Charges Garrison.

Generall Letter from the Deputy Governour and Councill of Fort St. David for the United trade dated 10th Instant now read.

Agreed that the President provides Ten Thousand Pounds worth of Allumgeer Pagodas to send to Bengall on the Tavestock, it being conformable to the Right Hon. United Company's Order.

> Thomas Pitt.
> William Fraser.
> Thomᵃ. Wright.
> Thom. Marshall.
> John Meverell.

The Commander of Ship Colchester had his despatch deliver'd him about 4 this evening, and at five he went off and said in the night.

Danes Sloop saild out of this road.

Dispatch'd pr. Pattamar a Generall Letter to the Deputy Governour, and Councill of Fort St. David dated this day. **16.**

Dispatch'd pr. an Armenian Cossed a Generall Letter to the Deputy Governour and Councill at Surat dated this day. **19.**

Brigganteen Destiny Thomas Edwards Master arriv'd in this road from Malacca.

Ship Samuel Mr. Holycross Master arriv'd in this road from Ganjam. **23.**

———FORT ST. GEORGE, FEBRUARY 1704———

ATT A CONSULTATION

Present

THURSDAY
24TH.

THOMAS PITT ESQ^R. PRESIDENT & GOVERNOUR.
WILLIAM FRASER   THOMAS WRIGHT
THOMAS MARSHALL   JOHN MEVERELL

Mr. Charles Bugden pays into the Right Hon. United Company's Cash the sum of Five hundred Pagodas in part of money collected from the Inhabitants for building the Black Town Wall and Works.

Agreed that Five Hundred Pagodas be advanc'd Mr. Thomas Marshall Paymaster towards building the Black Town Wall and Works.

Order'd that John Hunter be discharg'd from the Military of this Garrison it being his request, and that Peter Boyce and Gabriel de Costa Topasses be entertaind Souldiers.

Severall Letters to Metchlepatam, Vizagapatam, and Bengall all dated the 23^d Instant now read, and approv'd.

Order'd that the Accomptant draws out an Account of the Salary of those who have serv'd the United Company from the 22d July 1702 to the 25th of next Month.

Order'd that papers be putt upon the Sea and Choultry Gates to give notice that the Farms of Beetle Tobacco and Arrack will be lett to farm between this and the 15th next month from which time they are to commence, and that all people are free to come, and make their proposealls to the Governour for the same or the Governour and Councill on Thursday in every week.

There haveing been Notorious and egregious Villanies committed by the Heads of the Casts, in the unequall Assestment of the money for the Town Wall, in which they have not only lade great Sums upon some, and others go free, but in great measure have lain the burthen of the Tax upon the meanest and poorest sort of people whom they were strictly charg'd by the Governour, and Councill particularly to excuse so being desirous to be truly informd who and what has been the occasion of it, Tis order'd that Mr. William Fraser, Mr. Thomas Marshall, and Mr. John Meverell appoint convenient times for setting in the Town Hall and send for the Heads of the severall Casts, and all other Inhabitants as they think necessary, and their examin upon oath or otherways all matters relateing to that Affair, & report the same from time to time to ye Governr. & Councill.

Mr. Brewster Cheif Supra Cargo of Ship Strutham was before us this day, desireing that we would excuse him from paying Custom for what part of their Cargoe was sold here, urging severall reasons for the same to which he was answer'd to putt his request, and reasons in writeing, and we would consider of the same.

Tis agree'd that the Governour and Councill do meet to morrow morning at the sea Gate, when 'tis order'd that all the Grain Merchants attend there to view the new Measures made, by which 'tis intended all the grain that's bought and sold in this Town is to be measur'd by them and no other.

Mr. Coniers of the Gunroom Crew of this Garrison being very much given to drink, which occasion'd his neglecting his duty, for which the Governour severall months past stop't his pay, hopeing thereby to reclaim him, who having of late given some testimony of his reformation, and fair promises that he will persist in the same, therefore order'd that the Paymaster pays him his arrears.

Mr. Charles Bugden petitions to be discharg'd the Comp. service, haveing a design to settle at Acheen, wherein he desiees we would countenance and encourage him with the Company's Interest which accordingly was promis'd him and his Petition enter'd after this Consultation.

——*FORT ST. GEORGE, FEBRUARY 1704*——

Merss. Griffith and Bugden delivers in a Petition adviseing us also of their intentions of their Joint Settling at Acheen, and desire that they be countenanc'd, and encourag'd with the Company's Interest in those parts, which is promis'd them so far as wee find it consistant with their Honour, and Interest, their Petition is enter'd after this Consultation.

THOMAS PITT.
WILLIAM FRASER.
THOM^s. WRIGHT.
THOM. MARSHALL.
JOHN MEVERELL.

Honble. Sir,

Haveing a more than probable assureance of advanceing my fortune, by the assistance of some friends here, do make it my request (tho' indeed with some regret) to lay down the Honble. Company's service, after bringing up all business, provided I can gain your Hon^{rs}. &c^a. grant to settle at Acheen, and in consideration of above Eleven Years' faithfull dischargment of the severall employs committed to my charge; also that during my abode there my Honble. Patrons may have occasion to make use of me in the Place, which I shall most willingly obey, do further request a promise upon my returne thence, to be reinstated again in the Honble. Company's Service, or that you will please to represent the same home in my behalfe, wch. and all other favours shall be ever most gratefully acknowledged by.

Honble. S^r. &c^a.
Yo^r. most Obed^t. Hum^{ble}. Servt.
CHARLES BUGDEN.

FORT S^T. GEORGE,
23^D. FEB^{RY}. 170¾.

To HON^{BLE}. THOMAS PITT ESQ^R.
PRESIDENT AND GOVERN^R. FOR AFFAIRS
OF THE R^T. HON^{BLE}. ENGLISH EAST
INDIA COMP^A. ON THE COAST OF
CHOROMANDELL &C^A. COUNCILL OF
FORT S^T. GEORGE.

HON^{BLE}. S^R. &C^A.

Having encouragement from most of our freinds Traders of Place to settle for a while at Atcheen, we crave leave to proceed thither on Ship Stretham, and make bold to request the following perticulars, whereunto hope for your approbation and Consent.

That Your Hon^r. &c^a. will please to Grant (for the better countenance of our settling there) the Honble. Company's priviledges in that Port, with an authentick Copy of the severall Articles, as also a Letter of recommendation to the King and Government of that place.

That it may please your Hon^r. &c^a. to favour us with the liberty of living on the Hon^{he}. Companys grounds there, and to inclose, and build on the same such convenient Lodgings and Warehouses as shall be necessary at our own expense, for at pr n , 'ts open and a meer ruin, exposed to the incroachments of the natives and other Neighbouring thereabouts, who have begun to build Hutts and little shopps and may in time be totally Lost.

That Whereas all Shipping belonging to the English trading thither with the Company's Pass or not, Declare themselves to come from them, or at least to be protected by them, so consequently claim a right to their Priviledges, some whereof have abused them by paying Custome, and other unusuall impositions, to the prejudice of other Licensed Traders, Touching which we supplicate the Honble. Govern^r. would notifie to the Government what he shall think most for

——FORT ST. GEORGE, FEBRUARY 1704——

our Credit and the Publick good And to render us the more acceptable we shall prepare a handsome Present, such as has been usually given upon the like occasions, which desire may be in the Honble. Companys name.

And Lastly, That if your Honour &ca. shall please to favour us with a Grant of the premises, that you'l also further recommend us to the Gentlemen in Bengall, Surat &c^a. whence are sent Shipping yearly; And shall be ready on all occasions, & at all times to obey the Honble. Companys Commands to the utmost of our Abilityes, and in like manner to Testifie our gratitude to your Hon^r. &c^a. being

Your most obliged Hum^{ble}.
Servant^s to Command

FORT S^t. GEORGE,   HENRY GRIFFITH,
24th. FEB^{RY}. 1703/4.   CHARLES BUGDEN.

25TH.   Ketch Queen Anne M^r. Bulkley Master arrived in this road from Fort S^t. David.

27TH.   Ship Canturbury arrived in this road from the same place.

Ship Chambers Friggat Capt. Thomas South Comand^r. arrived in this road from China about 12 at noon, on whom came M^r. Dolben and M^r. Frederick who brought us a Pacquet from the Rt. Honble. old East India Comp^y. dated 17th. September 1701 as also delivered all their Bookes and Accounts relating to the Cargo of said Ship.

Ship Blessing Captain Thomas Branock Com^r. arrived in this road from China.

Sloop Gangees sailed out of this road for Atcheen.

AT A CONSULTATION

Present

TUESDAY. 29TH.

THOMAS PITT ESQ^r. PRESIDENT &c^a.
[Lacuna]   WILLIAM FRASER.
THOMAS WRIGHT.   THO^s. MARSHALL.
JOHN MEVERELL.   THOM^s. FREDERICK.
M^r. FRANCIS ELLIS *Sick.*

Thomas Pitt Esqr. as Mintmaster reads his Mint Account for the month of January last.

M^r. John Meverell Land Customer reads his Land Custom Accounts for the month of January last, vizt.

Choultry Custom	...	...	...	...	Pa. 95 : 35 : 21
Rubie Broakers	...	...	...	...	6 : 0 : 72
Town Brokers	...	...	...	...	1 : 28 : 60
Cutt Grass	...	...	...	...	1 : 3 : 27
Registring Slaves	...	...	...	...	= : 32 : ...

Pag. 105 : 2 : ...

Ordered that One Thousand Pagodas be paid Thomas Marshall Paymaster for defraying Charges Garrison.

The Governour produced a Paper sent by Kings Buxee to Cojee Gregoree an Armenian inhabitant in this Place, the purport of wch. is threats about our Towns, which Paper is Enter'd after this Consultation.

----*FORT ST. GEORGE, FEBRUARY 1704*----

M͟r. Thomas Wright Sea Customer reads his Sea Custom Account for the month of January last, Viz͟t.

To Custom on Goods Imported & exported. Pa.	2,986 :	3 :	—
To Custom on Grain	1,158 :	18 :	60
Anchorage	22 :	18 :	—
Salvage	4 :	— :	—

Pag. 4,171 : 3 : 60

Mess͟rs. Brewster &c͟s. Supra Cargoes of the Struthem delivered us in a Petition this day, desiring that they may be exempted from Paying Custom, alledging that their stock was but small in so much that they feard itt would little more then bear the Charge of the Ship, so that by lessening the stock it increased the charge which being debated, and well consider'd 'twas agreed they should pay no Custom for such Goods as belonged *bona fide* to the Company, of which they are to give a Just Account and if required upon Oath. Their Petition is as entered after this consultation.

There being a Clock to be sold for Forty five Pagod͟s. and we wanting one for the head of the stairs. Ordered that the Paymaster do buy the same.

> THO. PITT.
> WILL: FRASER.
> THO: WRIGHT.
> THOM͟s. MARSHALL.
> JOHN MEVERELL.
> THO͟s. FREDERICK.

FROM THE BUXEE TO COJEE GREGOREY.

Sheik Abdasalam has wrote Doud Cawnn in the following manner, That the Villages which Assed Cawn, and Cawn Bahaudear had given to the Governour of Chineapatam, Cawn Bahaudear had now given one or two of them to Doud Cawns Jaggeer, but the Governour's servants refuse to lett him take possession thereof, upon which I discoursing Doud Cawn he returned Sheik Abdasalam the following answer: Till I incamp in those parts I would not have you meddle with the matter only tell the Governour that his servants had best be quiet, and make no disturbance betwixt us; and upon my arrivall in those parts, I will take notice of mine and Cawn Bahaudear's Jaggeer and will satisfie the Governour about it, so I have spoken to Cawn Bahaudar's officers not to meddle anything in it till my arrivall at S͟t. Thoma, and this I advise you.

FOR THE HON͟ble. THOMAS PITT ESQ͟r.
PRESIDENT FOR THE AFFAIRES OF THE HON͟ble.
ENGLISH EAST INDIA COMPANY AND
GOVERN͟r. OF FORT S͟t. GEORGE AND FORT
S͟t. DAVID, & THE COAST OF CHOROMANDELL
&c͟a. COUNCILL.

HON͟d. S͟rs.

When first we designed for this Port of Madrass, we had a prospect of making a voyage for the United English East India Company but since our arrival here, do find it to come much short of our expected Proffit, part of the Cargo not selling for the first cost, as likewise do understand by the Captain of our Ship, that wee shall be obliged to supply him with a much larger sume then what is designed in Charter Party, our Ship being ill fitted out of England with stores and necessarys for a trading voyage, especially sailes which is one of our chiefest wants as well as Provissions, this last was occasioned by our throwing half over-board in our outward bound passage, it not being fitting to eat, of which we

——FORT ST. GEORGE, FEBRUARY 1704——

acquainted the Honble. Company in our last: For the reasons aforesaid we the Supra Cargo of the Ship Strutham do humbly request your Honours to demaind no Custom for our Cargoe brought hither, if otherwayes 'twill be a great lessening to the designed stock the Honble. Company intended for a trading Voyage this we humbly recommend to your Honours consideration and in the mean time beg you to believe that we are with all due respects.

Hon^d. S^rs.

Yo^r. Hon^rs. most faithfull & obedient Serv^ts. to Command

CHAR. BREWSTER.

WILLIAM DANIEL.

FEBRUARY 28TH. 170$\frac{3}{4}$.

MARCH pmo.

Received ⅌ Pattamars a Generall Letter from the Deputy Governour and Councill of Fort S^t. David dated 28th. the past month.

AT A CONSULTATION

Present

WEDNES-
DAY pmo.

THOMAS PITT ESQ^R. PRESIDENT & GOVERNOUR.

THOMAS WRIGHT.	WILLIAM FRASER.
JOHN MEVERELL.	THOMAS. MARSHALL.
THOM^s. FREDERICK.	M^r. FRANCIS ELLIS, *sick*.

Generall Letter from the Deputy Governour & Council of Fort S^t. David dated 28th. February now read.

The R^t. Honble. United Company having ordered ten Thousand Pound sterling to be sent to Bengall in gold or silver, the latter being dear and difficult to be gott 'twas Agreed that the same should be sent in Allumgeer Pagodas, but the President acquainting us this day to that Amount was not procureable in Town, and with his utmost endeavours he had been able to get no more then Eleven Thousand one Hundred Pagodas which is agreed to be delivered the Warehouse-keeper and that the remainder with the approbation of the Assay Master be bought up in China Gold.

THO: PITT.

[*Lacuna*].

WILL. FRASER.

THO^s. FREDERICK.

THO: WRIGHT.

THOM^s. MARSHALL.

JOHN MEVERELL.

2ND

Dispatch'd ⅌ Pattamars the following Packets Viz^t.

To M^r. William Tillard at Metchlep^m. dat^d. 28th. past mo^th.

Two Packets to Vizagapatam for the seperate and United Trade of Ditto date.

3RD

Ketch Heirusalem Coja Mark Noquedah arrived in this road from Bengall.

Ship Allebux sailed for Narsapore.

4TH

The following order was signed by the Governour and Council Viz^t.

The Deputy Governour and Council of Fort S^t. David having in their two last Letters wrote us the great want they are in for money to defray the expences of their Garrison, earnestly desiring us to send them some. There being now an

——*FORT ST. GEORGE, MARCH 1704*——

opportunity by Padre Landon who sets out for that Place on Monday next, beleive it a safe conveyance to remit them Two Thousand Pagodas, to which your opinion is desired.

> THOMAS PITT.
> WILLIAM FRASER.
> THOMAS WRIGHT.
> THOMAS MARSHALL.
> JOHN MEVERELL.
> THOMAS FREDERICK.

Ship Presid^t. Capt. Greenhaugh Comand^r. arrived from Queddah.   5TH.

This day Padre Landon set out for Fort S^t. David with whom was sent 6TH.
the Two thousand Pagodaes as agreed on the 4th. Instant, and Twenty Rashpootes was sent with him as a Guard as Far as ffort S^t. David.

AT A CONSULTATION

Present

THOMAS PITT ESQ^R. PRESIDENT & GOV^R.
[*Lacuna*]   WILLIAM FRASER.   MONDAY
THOMAS WRIGHT.   THOMAS MARSHALL.   6TH.
JOHN MEVERELL.   THOMAS FREDERICK.

M^r. Thomas Marshall Paymaster reads his Paymaster's Account for the month of January last Viz^t.

Charges Garrison ...	...	...	...	Pa. 1303 :	6 : =
Charges Cattle ...	...	...	...	90 :	30 : =
Silk Worms ...	...	...	...	11 :	13 : =
Account Presents ...	...	...	...	6 :	2 : =
Factors Provissions	...	...	...	10 :	6 : =
Charges Dyet ...	...	...	...	642 :	14 : =
Charges Generall ...	...	...	...	379 :	= : =
Fortifications and repairs	...	...	...	156 :	12 : =

Pag.   259 : 11 : =

And it is agreed that One Thousand Pagod^s. be advanc'd him towards defraying Charges Garrison.

Agreed that the President payes out of Cash Eleven Thousand two hundred and four Pagodas, being Amount of China Gold bought, and delivered the Warehousekeeper to be sent to Bengall on Ship Tavestock.

Capt. Heron being at Policherry when the French released the Prisoners taken on the Canturbury, who wanted where withall to subsist them in their way to this Place, upon which he distributed amongst them Thirty four Pagod^s. which is ordered to be repaid him by the Paymaster and that he gives him our thanks for his compassion on the poor men.

Ordered that Thomas Sammon be Entertaind as Cooke of the Fort at Five Pagod^s. ₱ Mensem.

Agreed that Fifty Pagodas be paid Mannangapah for six months Town Conicoply's duty ending ult^o. Jan^{ry}. last.

The President produces a sawsy Letter he received yesterday from the Chief Junkaneer Mootombee Moodelaree which is Enter'd after this Consultation.

About 7 this morning M^r. Francis Ellis dyed, having lain a long time

——*FORT ST. GEORGE, MARCH 1704*——

ill, who left M^r. Thomas Wright and M^r. George Lewis his Trustees, the former producing his Will, which was read in Consultation.

Ordered that M^r. Edward Rawdon be Entertaind as Doct^{rs}. Chief mate at Five Pagod^s. ⅌ Mensem.

> THO. PITT.
> WILL. FRASER.
> THO. WRIGHT.
> THOM^s. MARSHALL.
> THOM^s. FREDERICK.
> JOHN MEVERELL.

FROM MOOTOMBEE JUNCKANEER.

I received your kind letter wherein you mention of having firme Perwannas for the villages and also of having dearly paid for them and that you design never to part from them, without you are reimbursed your money, what you write concerning Perwannas is true, but the Duan who is our master and has full Power over the Karnauduck country we are obliged to obey, I doubt not but that your Hon^r. is sensible that Tyher Cawn and the Phousdar of Pullemullee have received Perwannas relating to the said Towns I have frequently received Letters from Zypher Cawn, whereby I understand that he intends to join with me, but have desired him and the Phousdar for Pullamullee to have two or three dayes more patience, esteeming it as a kindness done to your Honour I am obliged to obey their orders, but the reason why I thus long have delay'd them is for the esteem I bear to your Honour and kindness to your Inhabitants. I was in hopes that your Honour long before this would have found out means to have cleared me of this bussiness, but find to the contrary. Check Abdee Sallam is lately arrived here, who showed me the Perwannas he has received about the Townes, when I showed him them I had received who answered that we must be obedient to our Masters orders, which is the reason of my writing to your Honour to send one of your vackeels to Satisfie the Phousdar, we shall not then be wanting to write to our Masters in your Honour's behalf, peace being the only thing we desire, but in the mean time you may order my people to take possession of the Villages out of which I am informed your Honour has ordered all the Paddy to be carryed, which order you must Countermand without delay receiving dayly Perwannas from our Masters which we must be obliged to putt in execution what can I write more.

7TH. Received a Generall Letter from the Generall and Council of Suratt dated the 15th November last, and from the Commodore and Council at Anjengo dated the primo February last.

8TH. Ship Tavestock Capt. Matthew Martin Commander sailed for Bengall, by whom sent the following Packets Viz^t.

To the Council for the United Trade dated the 24th February and 7th March 1703-4.

To President Board &c^a. Council in Bengall dated the 23rd. February last.

To S^r. Edward Littleton &c^a. Council at Hugley dated the 24th. February last.

Ship Allfaunde arrived in this road from Mergee Capt. Mare Comander.

Ship Sta. Cruize Senh^r. Ignatius Comander arrived in this road from Manilha.

9TH. Ship Allemud Mooseeraude Noquedah arrived in this road from Bengall.

————FORT ST. GEORGE, MARCH 1704————

At a Consultation

Present

THOMAS PITT ESQ^R. PRESIDENT & GOV^R.
WILLIAM FRASER.   THOMAS WRIGHT.
THOMAS MARSHALL.   JN°. MEVERELL.
THOMAS FREDERICK.

FRIDAY
10TH.

Generall Letter from the Generall and Councill at Surat dated 15th. November, and from Comodore &c^a. Council of Anjengo dated p^{mo}. February last.

Thomas Pitt Esqr. President reads his Accounts of the R^t. Honble. United Companys Cash for the month of February last, Ballance Pag^s. 54726 : 34 : 4.

An answer to Mootumbee's Saucy Letter was now read, and Enterd after this Consultation.

Few dayes past here coming to Town a Moor man who has a very considerable Employ under the King in these parts and esteemed a Friend to the English, so that to preserve his Friendship; 'Tis agreed that the President gives him the following Present Viz^t. 6 Y^{ds} Scarlet, one Guilt sword, looking Glass, and 2 bottles rosewater.

There being a vacancy in this Councill by the death of M^r. Ellis, 'Twas proposed by the President to fill it up with M^r. Robert Raworth for the following reasons. First That the Company had particularly showed a regard they had for him by making of him a Merchant, and ordering him to reside in this Place. Secondly. That he is the only new Company's servant here. Thirdly. 'Tis to be inferred from the settlement of the United Affairs in Bengall, that the Managers desire an equall number of the old and new Company's servants to be in the mannagement of the United Affairs. Fourthly and Principally that M^r. Raworth appears to be a sober, Dilligent, & Ingenious man, and by his deportment promises to be a usefull and Profitable servant to the Company. 'Tis resolved that the consideration of filling up the Council be deferred to another meeting.

The Governour acquaints that Peter de Pomera has offered Three thousand five Hundred Pagod^s. ⅌ Annum for the Arrac Farme, and beleives can be brought to more, and desires the Council to meet tomorrow morning at the Garden House to fix the same the month expiring the 15th. Instant.

The death of M^r. Ellis occasioning a General alteration in the employments of the Gentlemen of the Council, 'Tis ordered as follows, and to Enter upon their Employes the primo next month.

M^r. William Fraser Second, and to take charge of the Bookes.

M^r. Thomas Wright Third, to take charge of the Warehouse to whom M^r. Fraser is to surrender the same.

M^r. Thomas Marshall Fourth, to take charge of the Sea Customs, to whom Mr. Wright is to deliver the same.

M^r. John Meverell Fifth and Paymaster to whom M^r. Marshall as soon as clears that account delivers him the Bookes.

M^r. Thomas Frederick Sixth, and Land Customer to whom Mr. Meverell is to deliver up the same.

THO. PITT.
WILLIAM FRASER.
THO^s: WRIGHT.
THOM^s. MARSHALL.
JOHN MEVERELL.
THOM^s. FREDERICK.

c-]

------FORT ST. GEORGE, MARCH 1704------

To Mootombee Cheif Junckaneer.

I received your Letter and observe the contents, Our resolutions about the Towns for which we have so firme Pirwannas; besides paid Dearly for 'em, you have been often acquainted with and now tell you again we will never part from them without we are reimburst our money, and none expect we should but such as have shook hands with honour and Justices.

I never owned any Goods that were comeing into this place, but such as belonged to us, and for our Inhabitants 'tis alwayes my charge to them that they pay the Kings Dutys according to Sallabad and no other in which I will protect them; as this, you may also take as you please.

Thómas Pitt.

SATURDAY 11TH.

AT A CONSULTATION

Present

Thomas Pitt Esqr. President & Govern¹.
WILLIAM FRASER.   THOMAS WRIGHT.
THOMAS MARSHALL.   JOHN MEVERELL.
THOMAS FREDERICK.

This day we had the old Arrao Farmers, and Peter de Pomera before us, the latter bid 3600 Pagª. ₱ Annum for the Arrac Farme, and the others not willing to give so much, 'Tis agreed he should have it; and the Secretary ordered to draw out a Lease of the same for Five yeares to commence from the 15th. Instant, and the said Pomera to pay his Rent monthly, the Lease for which is as enter'd after this Consultation.

THO. PITT.
WILL: FRASER.
THO: WRIGHT.
THOMª. MARSHALL.
JOHN MEVERELL.
THOS. FREDERICK.

Locus Sigile

WE THE PRESIDENT AND COUNCIL OF FORT Sʳ. GEORGE FOR AFFAIRES OF THE Rʳ. HONᴮᴸᴱ. UNITED ENGLISH EAST INDIA COMPANY, do Grant unto Peter de Pomera aingarapah Venketadry, Peria Virapa, Musell Taunapa &cª. Partners the Licence for Distilling Arrao and selling Arrack by retail, and the Licence of buying and selling Arrac Root for one year commencing the fifteenth March 170¾ and ending the 15th. of March 170⁴⁄₅ forbidding all other Persons to Distill Arrao or to sell by retail, or to buy or sell Arrac root in Fort St. George Madrassapatam or the Liberties thereof, without licence first obtain'd of the said Peter de Pomera &c under penalty of forfeiting to the Rᵗ. Honᵇˡᵉ. Company all Arrac so distilled, or sold by retail, and the Arrac root bought or sold, and satisfying the damages accruing to the said Peter de Pomera &c., as the justices of the Choultry shall see cause to award. The said Peter de Pomera &cª. observing conditions and orders, Vizt.

1. The said Peter de Pomera &cª. are to pay the Honᵇˡᵉ. United Companys Cash on the Fifteen [of] every month next after the Date hereof, dureing the said term of Five years The sume of Three hundred Pagodas.

——FORT ST. GEORGE, MARCH 1704——

2. They are to cause the Arrac to be well distilled of wholsome Ingredients, under the penalty of suffering the punishment formerly provided again the use of of Dutrow.

3. They are to Register in the Land Customers Bookes the Persons to whom they shall Grant Licences by Virtue hereof.

4. Those who take Licences from the said Peter de Pomera &cª. for selling Arrac by retail, are subject to such penaltyes and Punishments as have been formerly declared for misdemeanours, and offences committed against the orders of the Garrison.

5. The said Peter de Pomera &cª. shall not sell or make over any part in the said Farme to any Person wt.soever without leave first obtained from the President and Council for so doing.

6. The said Peter de Pomera &cª. are to deal reasonably wth. such Persons as Import Arrac root by Sea or Land, and if the Importers thereof shall complain to the Justices of the Choultrey, the said Peter de Pomera &cª. are to Act according to their Determination, as well in that as in all differences which shall arrise between them and others, or among themselves in any manner relating to the Arrac Farm. Given under our Hands, and the seal of the Rt. Honble. Company this Fifteenth day of March 170¾.

> THOMAS PITT.
> WILLIAM FRASER.
> THOMAS WRIGHT.
> THOMAS MARSHALL.
> JOHN MEVERELL.
> THOMAS FREDERICK.

AT A CONSULTATION

Present

THOMAS PITT ESQ^R. PRESIDENT & GOVERNOUR.
WILLIAM FRASER. THOMAS WRIGHT.
THOMAS MARSHALL. JN°. MEVERELL.
THOMAS FREDERICK.

THURSDAY 16TH.

Mr. Joseph Hiller Provissional Storekeeper reads his Storekeepers Accounts for the months of January and February, and payes into the Rt. Honble. United Company's Cash Two Hundred Pagodas on account of Stores sold.

Mr. John Meverell Land Customer reads his Land Custom Account for the month of February last.

Choultry Custom	...	...	...	...	Pagª: 106: 8: 45
Rubie Broakers	...	...	...	...	25: 11: 20
Town Broakers	...	...	...	...	5: 2: 76
Registring Slaves	...	...	...	...	= 8: 0

Pagª. 236: 2: 4

Agreed that One Thousand Pagodas be paid Mr. Thos: Marshall Paymaster for defraying Charges Garrison.

Ordered that John Emas be Entertain'd one of the Gunroom Crew in this Garrison.

——*FORT ST. GEORGE, MARCH 1704*——

The R^t. Hon^{be}. United Company having on Ship Tavestock a parcell of course Hatts supposing they intended them for the souldiers of this garrison who all wear Granadeer Caps, and they being very lyable to be dammaged by the moth, ordered that Storekeep^{rs}. do sell the same at Outcry.

Governour produced Translate of a saucy Letter received yesterday from the Governour of Sta. Thoma and proposes an answere thereto, which was read & approved, Copyes of both are as Enterd after y^e. Consultatⁿ.

> Tho: Pitt.
> Will: Fraser.
> Tho: Wright.
> Thom^s: Marshall.
> John Meverell.
> Thos. Frederick.

FROM MIRUSMAUN PHOUSDAR.
OF S^r. THOMA.

I have power over Chinapatam and likewise over S^t. Thomas, as it belongs to the King, whose Grant of Chinapatam Ground to the Company was on no other intent then to make the Place fruitfull, and bring riches into his Kingdom, but not to Act any thing that should prove unjust or prejudicial to the Merchants Interest there. I can't help putting you in mind of the Governours of Golcondah and Vizapore, who for their unjust actions, and ill behaviour were instantly turned out of their Province, notwithstanding all their resistance and clapt into Irons, what reason therefore has the King to value any one, seeing he turns out whosoever he pleases, and who by his Great kindness and Justice towards his people has obtaind of God to conquer wheresoever he comes, and knowing me to be one of his officers, I wonder at the style you write me, what can I say more—

To MIRUSMAUN PHOUSDAR OF S^r. THOMA.

I received your impertinent and insolent letter, wee all know your King to be Great, wise, and just and many of his Nobles Persons of Great Honor but most of his little Governours amongst who^m. I reckon you, very uncorrupt and unjust. We would have you to know we are of a Nation whose sovereign as great and Powerfull, able to protect his subjects in their Just rights over all the world, and revenge whatever injustices shall be done them, of which there will be speedy Instances given, I am not a little surprised at your saucy expressions, as well as actions in Imprisoning my Inhabitants, when you know I can fetch you hither and correct you for both, this is an answere to your Letter.

> THOMAS PITT.

22^D. Received ℀ Pattamars a Generall Letter from William Tillard at Metchle-patam dated the 13th. Instant.

AT A CONSULTATION

Present

THURSDAY
23^D.

THOMAS PITT ESQ^R. PRESIDENT & GOVERN^R:
WILLIAM FRASER.   THOMAS WRIGHT.
THOMAS MARSHALL.   JOHN MEVERELL.
THOMAS FREDERICK.

Thomas Pitt Esqr. as Mintmaster reads his Mint Accounts for the month of February last, and payes into the R^t. Honble. United Companys Cash the sume of Two hundred and thirty Pagodas seventeen fanams and forty Cash, as the Ballance of that Account.

——*FORT ST. GEORGE, MARCH 1704*——

Ponagette Narso &cᵃ. Tobacco and Beetle farmers pays into the Rᵗ. Honᵇˡᵉ. United Companys Cash the sume of Six hundred and fifty Pagodas on that Account.

Gruapah &cᵃ. Arrac Farmers payes into the Rᵗ. Honᵇˡᵉ. United Companys Cash the sume of Three hundred Pagodas on that Account.

Mʳ. Thomas Wright Sea Customer payes into the Rᵗ. Honourable United Companys Cash the sum of One Thousand Pagodaes on Account Sea Customs.

This day was the Lease for the Arrac Farme deliverd to Peter de Pomera who was strictly charged to observe the same, and that he put nothing into the Arrac that was destructive to the health of the People, more especially Dutrow.

> Tʜᴏ : Pɪᴛᴛ.
> Wɪʟʟ : Fʀᴀꜱᴇʀ.
> Tʜᴏ : Wʀɪɢʜᴛ.
> Tʜᴏᴹˢ. Mᴀʀꜱʜᴀʟʟ.
> Jᴏʜɴ Mᴇᴠᴇʀᴇʟʟ.
> Tʜᴏˢ. Fʀᴇᴅᴇʀɪᴄᴋ.

Ship Malborough Capᵗ. Minter Master Sail'd this morning out of this road 25ᴛʜ. for Emoy in China by whom sent a Generall Letter to the Generall and Councill of Battavia dated the 23ᵈ. Instant, to be forwarded by the first opportunity from Malacca, and also to the Supra Cargoes of Ship Sidney, inclosing therein a price Current of China Goods on this Coast.

Ship Commerce Mʳ. Henning Master arrived in this road from Bengall, by 26ᴛʜ. whom received a Generall Letter from President Beard &cᵃ. Councill datᵈ. 10ᵗʰ. and 12 Feby.

Received ℗ Pattamars a Generall Letter from Mʳ. William Tillard at Metchle-patam dated 15ᵗʰ. Instant.

AT A CONSULTATION

Present

Tʜᴏᴍᴀꜱ Pɪᴛᴛ Eꜱqᴿ. Pʀᴇꜱɪᴅᴇɴᴛ ᴀɴᴅ Gᴏᴠᴇʀɴᴿ.   Mᴄɴᴅᴀʏ
   Wɪʟʟɪᴀᴍ Fʀᴀꜱᴇʀ.   Tʜᴏᴍᴀꜱ Wʀɪɢʜᴛ.   27ᴛʜ.
   Tʜᴏᴍᴀꜱ Mᴀʀꜱʜᴀʟʟ.   Jᴏʜɴ Mᴇᴠᴇʀᴇʟʟ.
       Tʜᴏᴍᴀꜱ Fʀᴇᴅᴇʀɪᴄᴋ.

Generall Letter from Mʳ. William Tillard at Metchlepatam dated 15ᵗʰ. Instant now read.

The Chambers Friggat calling in at Pollicondore as she came from China, where Mʳ. Dolben tells us he received a Letter from the Deputy Governour and Council there, Directed to the Governour and Council here, which has mett with the misfortune to be lost, supposing it was thrown overboard when they mett with the French, but having read it he in good part remembers the purport thereof, which he was desired to put in writing, and accordingly did it, being a request to us, to furnish them with slaves, stores &cᵃ. wᶜʰ. altho' we have no orders for the same from yᵉ. Mannagers for the United Trade, yet considering here being in Port, at this time a ship of theirs called the Strutham bound for China, which intends to call at that Island : that the following stores be sent on her, not doubting the Company will approve thereof.

Stript Gingham	...	...	...	...	... Peices	100
Moorees ordinary	...	...	...	...	... Bale	1
Blew Longcloth	...	...	...	...	... Peices	100
Shoes	...	...	...	...	... Pair	50
Stockings	...	...	...	...	... „	50

————FORT ST. GEORGE, MARCH 1704————

Working Tools	...	...	...	...	...	[*lacuna*]
Country Powder	...	...	...	...	... Candy	10
Hatts...	...	...	...	...	...	50
Saker Shott ...	...	...	...	...	...	200
Limejuice 50 or 60 Gallons			...	...	...	
Butter	...	...	...	...	... Jarrs	10

what slaves procureable and to write to Fort St. David to get some.

Henry Davenport Secretary Payes into the R⁺. Honble. United Companys Cash the sume of One Hundred and six Pagodas for purmission of Passengers on board Colchester.

M^r. William Fraser Warehousekeeper payes into the R⁺. Honble. United Companys Cash Fifteen hundred Pagod^s. on Account Goods sold.

The Governour acquaints the Council that whereas they had all heard that Coja Timore an Attorney for an Armenian in Persia, upon which Account he had great demands on Coja Awan, who delaying to adjust the same, took a Warrant out of the Court against him upon which Coja Awan delivered some Papers seal'd up to Coja Gregoria, who lodged them in the Court but soon after Coja Timore having business which occasion'd his going to S⁺. Thoma, whither he was followed by Coja Awan, where he prevaild by some indirect means or other with the Governour of that Place to seize Coja Timore and put him in Irons, and remain'd there himself, for which reason and they being two of our Inhabitants, He sent yesterday the Mulla and Brahminy to demand them and to have his positive answer whether he would deliver them, who when returned acquainted him that the Governour of Sta. Thoma insisted on a Cowl or Pardon for Coja Awan, and that the Papers lodged in the Court should be sent to him, the former was acquiese'd to but the latter with scorn rejected : This business occasioned great debates, and methods proposed for the revenging the onsolence of the Governour of S⁺. Thoma in seizing our Inhabitants, for that we considering the ill conse-quences of it, which will be, that no matters for the future shall be prosecuted here, but that him against whom the cause is carryed will appeal to S⁺. Thoma, the farther consideration of this is referred to another meeting.

THO. PITT.
WILL: FRASER.
THO: WRIGHT.
THOM^s. MARSHALL.
JOHN MEVERELL.
THO^s. FREDERICK.

———————

THURSDAY :
30TH.

AT A CONSULTATION

Present

THOMAS PITT ESQ^R. PRESIDENT AND GOVERN^R.

WILLIAM FRASER.	THOMAS WRIGHT.
THOMAS MARSHALL.	JOHN MEVERELL.
THOMAS FREDERICK.	ROB^T. RAWORTH.

Ordered that John Philips be Entertaind one of the Gunners Crew in this Garrison.

M^r. William Fraser Warehousekeeper reads his Warehouse Accounts for the months of January & Feb. last.

Ordered that One Thousand Pagodas be paid Mr. Thomas Marshall Pay-master for defraying Charges Garrison.

Ordered that Joseph Parker be discharged from farther service in this Garrison, and that John Pool be in his roome.

Ordered that Abraham Malay, Isaack Malay, and Dundee Madrass be Entertained as souldiers in this Garrison.

Ordered that the Paymaster loads on the Chambers Friggat for Bengal all the black stone he [has by him] according to a former request from the President & Council there to provide it for [their Chappel] This day was unanimously resolved to [fill up the Councill to the] Number of seven with M[r]. Raworth, there being a vacansy by the Death of M[r]. Ellis, and in consideration of the reasons mentioned in our Consultation of the 10th. Instant and that he be Storekeeper.

The Beetle and Tobacco Farmers were again sent for before us, and demanded whether they were ready to clear their Accounts, and willing to continue the farm of Beetle and Tobacco, to which they made some hesitation, then desired till Monday next to consider what answer to give, which was accordingly Granted them.

> T[HO]: P[ITT].
> W[ILL]: F[RASER].
> T[HO]: W[RIGHT].
> T[HOMAS] M[ARSHALL].
> J[OHN] M[EVERELL]
> T[HOM][s]. F[REDERICK].
> R[OBERT] R[AWORTH].

Ship Mahomudde, Mahomud Tyre Noquedah arrived in this Road from Quedda.

Sloop Diana M[r]. Nevell Master arrived in this road from Bombay.

A[PRIL] 3RD.

————

A[T] A C[ONSULTATION]

Present

> T[HOMAS] P[ITT] E[SQ][R]. P[RESIDENT] & G[OVERNOUR].
> W[ILLIAM] F[RASER].   T[HOMAS] W[RIGHT].
> T[HOMAS] M[ARSHALL].   J[OHN] M[EVERELL].
> T[HOMAS] F[REDERICK].   R[OB][R]. [R[AWORTH]].

M[ONDAY] 3RD.

M[r]. Thomas Marshall Paymaster reads his Account for the month of February Viz[t].

Charges Garrison	...	...	...	...	Pag[s]. 1,188: 3:
Charges Cattle ...	...	...	...	...	75: 3:
Silk Wormes ...	...	...	...	...	11: 9:
Charges Extraordinary ...	...	...	...	...	8: 21:
Charges Dyett	...	...	...	...	398: [25]
Charges Generall	...	...	...	...	347: [16]
Fort S[t]. David	...	...	...	...	2: [5]
Factors Provisions	...	...	...	...	2: [18]
Fortification and repairs	...	...	...	...	832: [15]
					Pa. 2,465: [21]

d

———*FORT ST. GEORGE, APRIL 1704*———

Agreed that Messrs. Meverell, Frederick and Raworth be Justices at the Choultry.

Agreed that one Thousand Pag^s. be paid M^r. John Meverell Paymaster for defraying Charges Garrison.

Ordered that M^r. Jeremiah Harrison be Receiver of the Sea Customs, and that M^r. Robert Raworth delivers to him all Bookes and Papers relating to [that Employ.]

M^r. Charles Bugden Rentall Generall payes into the R^t. Honble. United Companys Cash the summe of One Thousand and forty Pagodas and thirty four fanams Ballance Collected by him for Quitt Rents ending August 1702. And also reads his Scavengers Account for the year ending Ult°. September 1703 Ballance due to him Seaventy two Pag[odas] twenty three fanams which is agreed to be paid by M^r. H[unt] he farther payes One Hundred forty eight Pag^s. eight fanams and sixty Cash on Acco^t. Town Wall money.

Ordered that M^r. Richard Hunt be Rentall Gen^{ll}. and Scavenger, and to take charge of both the Employs from the primo Instant.

Ordered that Michael Fets be Entertained one of the Gunroome Crew in this Garrison.

Just as we was resolving to write to the Nabob about the Governour of S^t. Thomo seizing an Armenian Inhabitant of ours, thinking that the most proper way before we use violence in fetching him out of their hands, we just then received Letter from the Nabob and Buxie on the same subject. Translate of which are Enterd after this Consultation, upon which 'twas agreed they should be immediately answered.

> THO: PITT.
> WILL: FRASER.
> THO: WRIGHT.
> THOM^s. MARSHALL.
> JOHN MEVERELL.
> THO^s. FREDERICK.
> ROB^t. RAWORTH.

From Nabob Dowed Cawn. I am informed that one Coja Timore makes un[reasonable] demands on Coja Awan an Armenian Inhabitant of Chinapatam who has dwelt there a considerable time and am informed that you have set a Guard upon his house. [He] is a Person that does business for us, as we have [occasion] for Jewells, and stands indebted to us a consider[able Sum] of money, so that you would do well to order you[r People] by no meanes to meddle with him, and if there [are] any unreasonable Demands on him, I will accom[modate] the business when I arrive at Pianacaut [What can] I write more.

From the Buxee. I have been lately informed that one [Coja Timore] as Vackeel for another Person makes unreasonable [demands] on Coja Awan, and that your Honour has sett a[guard] upon his House which I wonder at, such unre[asonable]things are contrary to your Law, and cannot [but admire] that a Person must be ruined without exa[mination], if Coja Awan be indebted to any Person 't [will appear] against him, he is a Person that serves the [Nabob and]me with Jewells, and at this time is consider[ably] indebted to us, concerning which the Nabob has [wrote your] Honour, and I likewise write you as a [friend &] desire your Hon^r. to order that none of your [people] meddle with him or his effects, that he may [go on] quietly with our Affaires, and if there appeares any reasonable writings against him he shall satisfie the same according to reason and Justice, my family is at S^t. Thoma to whom I hope your Honour will be assisting, I shall shortly be in your Parts.

4th. Ship Dolphin Thomas Plumb master arrived in this road from Bengall by whom received a Generall Letter from the Council for the United Trade there dated 13th. Feb^{ry}. [last].

—— *FORT ST. GEORGE, APRIL 1704.* ——

AT A CONSULTATION

Present

THOMAS PITT ESQ. PRESIDENT & GOVERNOUR.
WILLIAM FRASER.   THOMAS WRIGHT.
THOMAS MARSHALL.   JOHN MEVERELL.
THOMAS FREDERICK.   ROBERT RAWORTH.

WEDNES-
DAY 5TH.

Letter to the Nabob, and another to the Buxie answer to what was received the second Instant, now read, and agreed to be sent. Copy of which as Entered after this Consultation.

THO: PITT.
WILL: FRASER.
THO: WRIGHT.
THOM. MARSHALL.
JOHN MEVERELL.
THOS. FREDERICK.
ROBR. RAWORTH.

Ketch Queen Anne Ralph Bulkly Master [arrived in] this road from Fort St. David, by whom received a Pacquet from the Deputy Governour and Council there dated 3d. Instant.

Ship Francisco arrived in this road from G[anjam] Sloop Vizagapatam Merchant arrived in yr. road from Ditto.

I received your Excellrs. Perwanna and [observe the]contents, by which I find that your Excellency [is mis] informed as to the affair between Coja Awan and Cojah Timore, both which Persons are our Inhabitants, yet nevertheless the Governour of St. Thoma[most unjustly] seized. Coja Timore and used him barborously [upon] a complaint of Coja Awans, grounded alto[gether] on falsityes, so with your Excellencys leave [I here] represent the truth to you. About two years [Past] there was here one Coja Paulo went to P[ersia on one] of our ships, who was Attorney for Coja Issop formerly an Inhabitant of this Place, who thô he left an [attor]ney yet recommended the care of his effects to our [Go]vernment desiring to assist his Attorney [on all occa]sions, this Coja Paulo dyed in Persia, who [left Cojah] Awan his Attorney here, by which means [he was] also Attorney to Coja Issuph who adjust [ed all] accounts with the deceased Coja Paulos [friends] in Persia and received from them an order to Coja Awan here to deliver to him or his order what effects left in his hands of his by Coja Paulo, to receive which as also all other effects in severall other parts, he sent this Coja Timore and two others, who arrived here about Ten months past, and soon after showing their Power to Coja Awan made their demands of the effects of Coja Issoph left in his Hands by Coja Paulo who readily promised before severall Persons to comply therewith, and some months after Coja Timore renewing his demands Coja Awan told him, that the effects were abroad on severall Voyages the obligations for which he was ready to deliver him up, deducting his Commission for the same, to which Coja Timore agreed and daily expected Coja Awans complyance, but he delaying it from month to month, Coja Timore &ca. complain[ed] to our Justice who ordered him to be taken into Custody or give security for his Person till the business was determined, upon which Coja Awan delivered into our Court of Justice some Papers sealed up, which to this day remain as they were, soon after which Coja Timore having business which occasioned his going to St. Thoma whither he was followed by Coja Awan who prevail'd with the Governour there (for reasons which are easily to be gues'd) to seize Timore put him in Irons and used him at a Barbarous rate, upon this Coja Awan remaind with that unjust

To NABOB
DOWED
CAWN
APRIL 4TH.
1704.

d-1

---FORT ST. GEORGE, APRIL 1704---

Governour which immediately occasioned severall of our Inhabitants to complain to me against him, he owing here to severall People between 6 : or 8000 Pag⁸ upon which I set a guard upon his House; that nothing might be [remov'd] till he returned and cleared these demands, I [a] few days [after] sent our Vacqueel to S⁺. Thoma to demand Coja Awan and Timore our Inhabitants, and would have [done it in] another manner, but for the reguard we have for your [Excell^{cy}.] resolving to apply ourselves to you before we [reverge] these injustices, and were writing you this Letter just as we received your Perwanna, by our Vacqueel [we offer'd] that whereas in this Place there are eminent [Merchants of] all Casts and Nations, that it should be decided [by such] as they should choose themselves, or upon a fair [and full] hearing in our Court of Justice, where all matters are [deter]mined according to the Law of God and man, an[d in no] Place but this, can this matter be decided, here [being all] three Witnesses, money, and Papers relating there[to, I offer'd] Awan my Cowle to returne hither, and end his [business] like a Merchant, when the Guard should be [taken off his] house, otherwise we would call sufficient [Witnesses at] the taking of an Inventory of what was [there and secure] it for the Payment of what he owes our Inhabitants but nothing of reason or justice would [satisfy him] and the ¦Governour of S⁺. Thoma, who [insisted on deli]vering back the Papers, which we can't part [with I have] here represented to your Excellency the whole truth of the matter not doubting but you will give [orders for the] delivering up to us our Inhabitants, having hitherto observed that you are a Lover of Honour and Justice I wish y^r. Excellenc^y all health and prosperity.

THOMAS PITT.

TO THE KING'S BUXEE—

APRIL 4TH
1704.

I received the Honour of your Perwanna & find that the Nabob and yourself are misinform'd in the business of Coja Awan and Coja Timore, a true relation of which I have sent the Nabob, a copy of which I here inclose to yourself which you may depend upon to be the truth, and in it you'll find how unjustly the Governor of S⁺. Thoma has acted in this matter, your Honour may remember how often yourself has wrote me not to protect the Inhabitants of S⁺. Thoma which I duely observed by making 'em return to their Habitations, your Family shall at all times command my assistance, I wish your Hon^r. health & prosperity.

THOMAS PITT.

AT A CONSULTATION

Present

THOMAS PITT ESQ^R. PRESIDENT & GOVERN^R.

THURSDAY
6TH.

WILLIAM FRASER.   THOMAS WRIGHT.
THOMAS MARSHALL.   JOHN MEVERELL.
THOMAS FREDERICK.   ROB^T. RAWORTH.

Generall Letter from the United Council at Fort William in Bengall dated 13th. February, and from Ditto dated 2^d. March both now read.

Ordered that the money pay'd into the R⁺. Honble. [United Comp⁸.] Cash for permission of Passage on board Ship Colchester be recharged, and brought to the old Company's Account it being for [money] due for Passengers going on [their Ship].

Thomas Pitt Esqr. President reads his [Account] of the R⁺. Honble. United Companys Cash for the [month of] March Ballance Pag⁸. 33309. 16. 1.,

Ordered that M^r. Stephen Frewen do coll[ect the] remaining part of the Town Wall money, and whereas M^r. Bugden was promised 100 Pag⁸. for [collect-

——*FORT ST. GEORGE, APRIL 1704*——

ing the] same, and did get in but part of it, for which he was allowed 25 Pag⁸. 'Tis agreed Mʳ. Frewen has the [remainder] 75 when he has collected the whole sūme.

Ordered that the Warehousekeeper delivers out pieces ordinary Broad cloth for the use of the old Compa[ny to be] paid at Invoice price.

Coja Awan that remains at Sᵗ. Thoma [owing a] considerable sūme to the Inhabitants of this place, the Court had ordered (by the advice and consent [of the Governour] and Council the Judge representing the same to us that his House should be open'd, and an [Intentory] taken of all Goods, and Household stuff in it in the presence of the Armenians, Mogulls and Pattans of this Place, who accordingly were summoned this day in order thereto, but instead of going to the house the Armenians and Mogulls came to the Governour the former desiring to be excused by reason they had effects in St. Thoma which would suffer thereby, the Mogulls alle[dg'd that the] Buxee's servant had been with them this [morning and] charged them in the Nabobs and his Masters names not to concern themselves in this matter, but the Pattans did not appear, they were ordered all to retire to the Town Hall, whilst the Governour and Council considered of it, who came to [the] following resolutions. That if any of the sufficient men of them would give security for Payment of Coja Awans debts, [or] delivery up of his Person within such a time as should be agreed on, or otherwise they must assist at the opening of his House and Godowns, and take an Inventory of all that was therein, to which if they did not agree, they must depart this Government with their Familys in three dayes time, so they were sent for and acquainted with the foregoing resolutions, the last of which did not a little startle them, and caused them to acquiesce with the following. That on Monday next there should meet at Coja Awans house Eight Armenians, eight Mogulls, eight Pattans, and eight Gentues, whose names were agreed on and that there [they were to] assist the Register of the Court to take an [Inventory] of all they found in the house and Godowns, which they were to attest under their Hands and Seals.

Mʳ. Hunt makes a report that the Account delivered in by Mʳ. Bugden of the Ground Rents and Scavengers agreed with the Generall bookes.

> Tho: Pitt.
> Will: Fraser.
> Tho: Wright.
> Thomˢ. Marshall.
> John Meverell.
> Thoˢ. Frederick.
> Robᵗ. Raworth.

Ship Sedgwick Capᵗ. Richard Rawlings Commander [arrived] in this road from Bengall by whom received the follo[wing pac]kets. From the United Council in Bengall, and [from the] President and Council there for the Seperate Aff[airs of the] old Company.

Ship Surat Merchant Capᵗ. Hancock Comʳ. arrived in [this]road from Pegue.
Ship Bomborupang arrived in this road from[. . .]
Ship Commerce Capᵗ. Bulkly Comʳ. sailed out of this [road for] Bengall.
Ship Sumarteen arrived in this road from Atcheen Cojah Woanes Noquedah.
Ship Latchme arrived in this road from Negapatam.
Ship Allemadutt saild out of this road for Bengall.

7.

9.

10.

11.

———FORT ST. GEORGE, APRIL 1704———

AT A CONSULTATION

Present

WEDNES-
DAY 12TH.

THOMAS PITT ESQR. PRESIDENT & GOVERNOUR.
WILLIAM FRASER.   THOMAS WRIGHT.
THOMAS MARSHALL.   JOHN MEVERELL.
THOMAS FREDERICK. ROBT. RAWORTH.

The Presidents Letter to the King of Atcheen dated the 11th. Instant, Instructions to Messr. Griffith and Bugden for a settlement at Atcheen, and a Commission to them to represent the Company in those Parts, all now read and approved, which are as Entered after this Consultation.

We knowing the Employ of the Secretary of this place to be very fatiguing, and his reward for the same to be much less here then in any other Parts of India, and that in all Places and by all Nations there are settled fees for a Secretary, we have therefore for the future encouragement of the Secretary of this Place settled the following Fees referring itt to the Honble. Mannagers for their approbation and confirmation of the same Vizt.

	Page.	fa.	ca.
Ships about 200 Tons	6	...	...
Ships of 200 or under	4	...	...
All Briggantines, Ketches and sloopes to be obliged to take a Pass for which to Pay ...	1	:	—
All Boats that saile with a Topsaile for a Pass, and to be obliged to take one	.	...	12
All Boats that saile without a Topsaile for a Pass and to be obliged to take one	:	—	9
Ships about 200 Tons a pass for their Men ...	4	:	—
Every single Person or Passenger that takes a Pass	2	:	—
All Cowles or Grants for Farmes Vizt.			
One Thousand Pags. and upwards value ℗ Annum	5	—	—
Five Hundred Pags. ℗ Annum Value ...	3	—	—
Under five hundred Pags. ℗ Annum Value ...	2		
Lieutenant for his Commission	4		
Ensign for his Commission	3		
For Registering of Diamonds every entry not exceeding 500 Pags. one Pago. under ...	0	:	18
For all orders to Commanders to receive Passengers on board ship for England	1	:	—
For Writing and Attesting and Certificate, order of Council or Paragraph of a Letter ...	:	—	18
For reading any Paper to the Governour & Council—Petitions or such like	:	—	18
For a discharge to any in the Garrison ...	:	—	6
For sending Letters by the Company's Pattamars Vizt.	[	. . .	]

Fort St. David fanam 1. Metchlepatam fanam 2. Vizagapatam fanam 4. Bengall fanam 6. Anjengo fanam 4. Surat fanam 9.

Ordered that Adrian Johnson be Entertained one of the Gunners Crew in this Garrison.

JOHN MEVERELL.   THO: PITT.
THOS. FREDERICK.   WILL: FRASER.
ROBT. RAWORTH.   THO: WRIGHT.
                       THOM. MARSHALL.

——*FORT ST. GEORGE, APRIL 1704*——

To his most Illustrious Majes[tie] Sultan Demollet Aulum, King of[Acheer] Thomas Pitt Esq. President for [Affairs] of the R. Hon. English East India Company [on the Coast] of Choromandell and Orixa and Governour of [Forts St. George] and S. Davids and City of Madrass &c. Wisheth Health.

May it please Y. Maj.

I heartily congratulate your Ma[jestie's] [accession] to the Crown, and wish that your Reign may be long and prosperous, for that we shall be always at your Majesty's service to do any thing that may contribute thereunto since your ascending the Throne we are informed that our Nation enjoyes their Ancient Priviledges in your Kingdom, which they were debarred of during the rebellious times, which Royall favours of your Majestie, have encouraged us to send this our Ship to your Port, on whom comes M. Griffith and M. Bugden to reside at our Ancient Factory, whom we desire may be favoured with yo. Royall Protection, and the free enjoyment of the English Priviledges.

We have sent by them a Present for your Majestie of which we beg your acceptance, as also our humble thanks for the bountys you have been pleased to bestow upon us, We wish your Majestie health and prosperity, and that you may be alwayes successfull against the enemyes to your Crown and Dignity, which shall be the hearty wishes of

                                    Your Maj. most Dutifull
 Fort S. George   & Obed. servant
 11th April 1704.   Thomas Pitt.

INSTRUCTIONS to Mess. Henry Griffith and Charles Bugden in order to their settling at Atcheen.

You having by your Petition to us dated the 24th. February, requested our Countenance and assistance in your design of settling at Atcheen (which Place is under the Direction of this Presidency) of which having duly consider'd we hereby Grant and order you to Act in the following manner.

First.

That on your arrivall at Atcheen you present the Presidents Letter to the King (of which we deliver you a Copy) with the Present you have obliged [yourselves] to carry at your own Charge, which must [go in the Right] Hon. Companys name.

Secondly.

That whereas the Hon. Company has a piece of Ground there, on which they formerly had [a factory] we hereby empower you to enclose the same [as you shall] think fitt, and build such necessary Houses and Warehouses as shall be most convenient for your accomodation but at no manner of charge to the Company.

Thirdly.

Whereas we here deliver you a Copy [of the Origi]nall Grant of the Priviledges in the Year 1660 [by the] Queen of Atcheen to the R. Hon. Company [which we] enjoyn you to have a particular regard to and to the utmost of your Power preserve, and if any [now residing] there, or that shall come from any part of [India of] English [birth] shall do anything towards the less [ening or] forefiting the same, do you advise us there of [that so they] may be prosecuted for it in such parts of [India where] they reside.

Fourthly.

We shall advise to Bengall and Surat of your settling at Atcheen by our permission and that we have empowered you there to represent the Company and call such to an Account as aforesaid as do anything to the prejudice of

——*FORT ST. GEORGE, APRIL 1704*——

their Priviledges, but for all other recommendation we hope you'l dese[rve by your] faithfull dealings, wth. those who make you [Consignments].

Fifthly.

We having a Warr with France and Spain, 'tis not impossible but that we shall have severall French Cruizers in those seas, and your Port as like as any to be their Place of Rendezvous, therefore order you that if any such Ships come to your Port, or that you hear of a certainty they are in those seas, or any Pyrats, that you with all speed dispatch advise thereof to Malacca, and all other Ports whither an opportunity presents of writing, for that you well knowing the seasons (that our Companys ships, and severall others belonging to this Coast, which are Generally of great value) when they come thro' the Streights of Malacca, and what charges you shall be att for your advices, we will by some meanes or other reimburse you, but caution you this, not to put us to any extravagant charge, we not knowing how to be repaid the same.

'Tis much to be fear'd that M^r. Delton who has resided a long time at Atcheen in contempt of the Companys Authority will be no Friend to your design, on whose actions you must make the best remarks you can and if you find, and have good proof thereof, that what he do's tends to the destruction of the Companys Priviledges, do you advise us thereof and we will give necessary orders therein, we earnestly recommend to you a frequent correspondence with this Place, when be sure to give full advices of all matters of importance. We wish you good success in your undertakings, and again recommend to you the intire preservation of the Com[panys] Priviledges, which you have promised shall [be done with] out any Charge to them Dated in Fort S^t. [George] this 12th. day of April 1704.

THO : PITT.
WILL : FRASER.
THOMAS WRIGHT.
THOMAS MARSHALL.
JOHN MEVERELL.
THOM[AS FREDERICK].
ROBERT [RAWORTH].

TO ALL TO WHOM THESE PRESENTS SHALL [COME] WE THE GOVERNOUR AND COUNCIL [OF FORT S^T.] GEORGE AND COAST OF CHOROMANDELL [FOR THE] R^T. HON^{BLE}. UNITED ENGLISH EAST [INDIA] COMPANY SEND GREETING.

THAT whereas we are informed [of great] disorders at Atcheen by severall English [that trade to] that Port, that tends to the ruin and destruction [of the] R^t. Honble. Companys Priviledges, to retrieve [which and to pre]serve them for the future we hereby empower [Messrs. Henry] Griffith and Charles Bugden to reside there [as the Companys] representatives, requiring all Her Majesty's subjects] Queen Anne of Great Brittain &c^a. to app[ly themselves] to the aforesaid Messrs. Griffith and Bugden [in all matters] and disputes between them and the Gov[ernment] who we hereby enjoyn to be assisting to them to the utmost of their Power. We also hereby empower the aforesaid Messrs. Griffith and Bugden to demand of all English Ships belongiug to any Port or Ports on this side Cape Bona Esperansa that Trade to Atcheen a view of their Passes which if they shall refuse shall be taken for Granted they have none, of which you are to advise the particulars, the Masters and Ships Name, and what Port she belongs to, and if any Pass be produced to you wherein if any thing mentioned is unusuall you are to take a Copy thereof attested and send it us by the first opportunity. We likewise hereby purmit the aforesaid Messrs. Griffith and Bugden to take Possession of the Ground belonging to the R^t. Honble. Company on which their

——*FORT ST. GEORGE, APRIL 1704*——

Factory formerly stood, to inclose the same and build such accommodations as they think convenient. Dated in Fort S^t. George 11th. April 1704.

> THOMAS PITT.
> WILLIAM FRASER.
> THOMAS WRIGHT.
> THOMAS MARSHALL.
> JOHN MEVERELL.
> THOMAS FREDERICK.
> ROBERT RAWORTH.

AT A CONSULTATION

Present

THOMAS PITT ESQ^R. PRESIDENT AND GOVERN^R.
WILLIAM FRASER.   THOMAS WRIGHT.
THOMAS MARSHALL.   JOHN MEVERELL.
THOMAS FREDERICK.   ROBERT RAWORTH.

THURSDAY
13TH.

Ordered that the Warehousekeeper sell Capt. Ignatius One Hundred Candy of Lead for Nine Pagodas ℔ Candy. Lead sold at 9 pag. per candy.

M^r. Charles Lockyer having Petitioned to be discharged the Companys service, Agreed that the same be granted him and his Petition Entered after this Consultation. Mr. Lockyer dismissed the Company's service at his request.

M^r. Thomas Wright Sea Customer reads his Sea Custom Account for the month of February [last, vizt.] Sea Customers Acco^t. read.

To Custom on Goods Imported and exported this

month	...	...	...	...	...	...	P^a. 3052 [13. 73.]
To Custom on Grain	...	...	...	...			244 [10. 44.]
To Anchorage	...	...	...	...	...		48 [18. .]

P^a. 3345 [6. 37.]

and payes into the R^t. Honble. Companys Cash [the summ] of one Thousand Pagodas on that Acco^t. Pa. 1000 pd. by him on y^t Acco^t.

Ordered that the Storekeeper do view [what Timber and] Plank is lately come from Pegue, and [report the] same to this board next Consultation, in [order to buy] in such stores of the same as shall be wanting. Storekeeper ordered to view some Timbers.

There being lately ordered that all Goods [brought in] by Land where they are Enter'd at the Choultry [and pay] two and a half ℔ Cent Custom, which when shipt off they pay Two and a Halfe ℔ Cent more, which w'd to be signified from the Land Customer to the [Sea Customer] by a Gentue Cajan, which is done now by [a certificate] in English, which occasions a great deal of [writeing] to him that attends the Land Customs, for whose incouragement. Tis ordered that what [certificates] he writes for Goods that their value is [from] five to Twenty five Pagod^s. shall pay halfe [a fanam, and] whatever surmounts that sume shall [pay one] Fanam. Fees to be allowed the Land Customers Assistant, and why.

This day the Farmers of Beetle and [Tobacco and] Arrack were before us, from whom was demanded the Payment of their Arrears, who answered that they had suffered much in the Farmes by Dowed Cawns coming to S^t. Thoma, and the Junckaneers frequent stoping of the Beetle, as also by our permitting severall Beetle Gardens to be planted within our bounds, which payes but halfe the Custom of that which comes from the Country, and severall other molestations they pretend from the Government which they say has been prejudiciall to them, for which they desire an allowance, and promise to pay the Ballance, 'Twas also Farmers of Beetle and [Tobacco] [before] the Presid^t. and [Council] & their Debt demanded.
[Sue for an] abatement.

e

Offer to [take
it at]
Pa. 6000.
per annum.

demanded of them whether they were willing to hold the Farme, to which they
seemed not very willing, but told us if they did they could give no more then six
Thousand Pagodas, upon which we answered that their month ended the seaven-
tenth Instant when [we] would take it into the Companys Hands, & accordingly
Mr. Frewen was sent for, and ordered to take charge of the same.

> Tho. Pitt.
> Will. Fraser.
> Tho. Wright.
> Thoms. Marshall.
> John Meverell.
> Thos. Frederick.
> Robt. Raworth.

At a Consultation

Present

Friday
14th.

Thomas Pitt Esqr. President & Governour.
William Fraser.   Thomas Wright.
Thomas Marshall.   John Meverell.
Thomas Frederick.   Robt. Raworth.

Halfe a
Yeares
salary due to
the Comps.
servts.
agreed to be
paid.

Mr. William Fraser as Accomptant does [now produce] an Account of salary
due to the Rt. Honble. Un[ited Companys] servants in this Place. Halfe salary
from [the 22d. July 1702 to] the 29th. September 1703, and from that time to
the 25th. March last whole salary Amounting to Pags. 2714. 13. [4. which is]
agreed to be paid out of Cash, in pursuance to the Manager's orders in their
Generall Letter ℗ Ship Tavestock [that] their servants shall be paid whole salary
in [the country] from the 22d. July 1702.

[Letters]
to severall
Places read
[and ap]
proved.

Generall Lettr. to the Deputy Governour [and Council] of Fort St. David, to
Mr. Tillard at Metchlepm. both [dated yester]day now read and approved.

[Pags. 2] 365
pd. into Cash
Accot. [Good]
sold out
of ye. Ware-
house.

Mr. William Fraser does now pay into the United Right Honble. Companys
Cash the sume of Two thousand [three] Hundred sixty five Pagodas on Account
Goods [sold out] of the Warehouse,

> Tho: Pitt.
> Will: Fraser.
> Tho: Wright.
> Thoms. Marshall.
> John Meverell.
> Thos. Frederick.
> Robt. Raworth.

Honble. Srs.

Your Honours Generosity and kind Inclination to promote the wellfare of
Youth incites me to trouble your Honour with an Affair of that Nature ; 'Tis what
you was pleased yesterday to speak of, which has wholy employ'd my thoughts
since, and Humbly offer 'em to your Honours prudent consideration.

As to the Honourable Company here are so many in their service better
capacitated then myself, and my Seniors that the mean service I can do them will
never be wanted, and the little hopes I have of advancing my small Fortune by
lying ashore and an opportunity now presenting, which gives me a fair prospect
of improving it, induces me to beg your Honours permission for going abroad, and

———*FORT ST. GEORGE, APRIL 1704*———

favourable assistance therein, since the improving my time well, and the experience I shall gain thereby will conduce much to the satisfaction of my Freinds, and enable me the better to serve your Honour when may be counted worthy your Commands.

[FORT ST.] GEORGE
APRIL 11TH. 1704.

Honble. Sr.

Yor. Honrs. Obedient hum[ble]
Servant

CHA : LOCKYER.

Ship St. Johan arrived in this road from Atcheen Coja Sattore Noquedah.   15
Ship Paula Doulat arrived in this road from [Bengall]

———

AT A CONSULTATION

Present

THOMAS PITT ESQR. PRESIDENT & [GOVERNOUR]   MONDAY
WILLIAM FRASER.   THOMAS WRIGHT.   17TH.
THOMAS MARSHALL.   JOHN MEVERELL.
THOMAS FREDERICK.   ROBERT RAWORTH.

Letter from Peddaway Duppa and Naggapau to the Governour and Councill now read. Ordered said [Letter be copy'd] and sent to Fort St. David for their answere. *Letter read*

Ponagetto Narso &ca. Tobacco and Beetle farmers pays into the Rt. Honble. United Companys Cash the sume [of Five] hundred and fifty Pagodas on that Account. *Pa. 550 pd. into Cash by the Tobacco Farmers.*

Agreed that the President payes the Warehou[sekeeper] Two thousand nine Hundred seaventy nine Pag. eleven fanams to buy 5,000 Rups. and to send the like Amount in pagodas to Vizagapatam, with all expedition, the Chief and Councill representing in their last Letter that their necessitys were very great on Account that the Nabob was expected there who expected a Present, and that they wanted [where with all] to defray the Charges of the Garrison and their servants and likewise to pay arrears for Rent to the [Nabob for] their Town. *P 2979: 11. ordered for Vizagapm.*

THO. PITT.
WILL : FRASER.
THOM : WRIGHT.
THOs. MARSHALL.
JOHN MEVERELL.
THOs. FREDERICK.
ROBT. RAWORTH.

Received ⅌ Pattamars the following Generals Vizt: —
From President Beard and Council datd. 16th. February last.
From the Chief and Council of Vizagapatam dated 16th. of February 6th. and 31st. March 1704
From Mr. Tillard at Metchlepatam datd. 4th. Instant.
Sloop Rawou Rautoon arrived in this road from Pegue.   18TH.

———

————FORT ST. GEORGE, APRIL 1704————

AT A CONSULTATION

Present

[WEDNES-
DAY] 19ᵀᴴ.

THOMAS PITT ESQ^R. PRESIDENT & GOVERN^R.
WILLIAM FRASER.   THOMAS WRIGHT.
THOMAS MARSHALL.   JOHN MEVERELL.
THOMAS FREDERICK.   ROB^T. RAWORTH.

**Pag^s. 1000
pay'd on
Acco^t.
Sea Customs**

M^r. Thomas Wright Late Sea Customer payes into y^e. R^t. Honble. United Companys Cash the sume of one Thousand Pagod^s. on Account Sea Customs.

**Paymaster
order'd to
pay Polli-
condore
Soldiers.**

There being severall Portuguez Souldiers willing to go to Pollicondore, ordered that the Paymaster advances to them Three months pay at two Pagod^s. ᵱ mensem, and that the steward layes in Provisions for them for the aforesaid time.

**Letter to
Vizag-
apatam.**

Generall Letter to Vizagapatam dated this day now read and approved ; and addition to Metchlepat^m. Letter.

**[1,000 Ps .]
Paid.**

Agreed that one Thousand Pagod^s. be paid M^r. John Meverell Paymaster to defray Charges Garrison.

**[Tobacco
and] Beetle
farmes lett
at 7,000
pag^s. per
annum.**

The Governour acquaints the Council that y^e. Tobacco and Beetle farmers had [offered seven] Thousand Pago[das] ᵱ Annum for the said Farme, to commence the same from the 17th. December, from which time their old Cowle expired, upon which the Farmers were sent for, who con[firmed] what the Governour had say'd, to whom 'twas[propo]sed by the Governour and Council that they s[hould hold] the Farmes to the 17th. next month, and [pay from 17th]

what terms.

December after the rate of seaven Thou[sand] pagodas ᵱ Annum, and that, in the mean time [if they settled] their Accounts to our satisfaction w[e would then] consider of giving them a new Cowle [for the Farm].

**Arrack
Farmers
Debt
demanded.

Sue
for an
abatement.

Why
[moie]ty of
their debt
excused.**

The Arrack Farmers were likewise sent [for who are in] arrears [*lacunae*] who insist [upon] having four months abatement as the Beetle and Tobacco Farmers had during Dowed Cawns besieging this Place who was answered that the Beetle and Tobacco farmes [desisted from] collecting those Reve-nues by order of the Govr. [&] Council, but to them was directed no such [orders, who] alledged they made, nor sold little or no arrac[during that]time by reason that most of the Inhabitants [deserted] the Place, and that they wanted some ingredi[ents which] were Generally imported from the Country, so that after a long debate it was unanimously agreed that [they] should pay a moiety of what they owed, or [life in pri]son till they did, and severity to be used to [compell them] thereto.

THO : [PITT].
WILL : [FRASER].
THO : WRIGHT.
THOMAS MARSHALL.
JOHN MEVERELL.
THO^s. FREDERICK.
ROB^T. RAWORTH.

20ᵀᴴ

Ship Dorothy Capt. [Rose] Commander sailed out of this road for Vizaga-pa[tam by] whom sent two packets to the Chief and Council there, one for the United Trade and the other for the Separate dated [15th. and 16th.] instant.

22

Huglyana Ketch [Charles Hop]kins Master arrived in this road from [Bengal by whom] received a generall letter from the Uni[ted Councill] there dat^d. 4th. & 6th. March last.

———FORT ST. GEORGE, MAY 1704———

The following order [was signed] by the Governor and Council Ordered that 24
the [Warehouse keeper] immediately unload all the salt Petre a[nd Rice
come] on the Huglyana Ketch (from) Bengal on the [Right Honble.
United]Companys acct^t.

> THOMAS PITT.
> WILLIAM FRASER.
> THOMAS WRIGHT.
> THOMAS MARSHALL.
> JOHN MEVERELL.
> THOMAS FREDERICK.
> ROBERT RAWORTH.

Ship Stretham Capt. [Thomas] Flint Commander sailed out of this road for 25TH
Fort [S^t. David] from thence designed for China.

Ship Chambers Frigat, Capt. Thomas South Commander sailed out of this 26TH
road [for Bengall] by whom sent two packets one for the [United Council] and
the other for President Beard etc. [Council] for the Separate Affairs.

Ship Prince Charles [belonging to] the Royall Danish [Compy.] sailed out of
[this road for 'T'r]incombar.

Received ⅌ Pattamar [via Metchlepatam] a Generall Lett^r. from the Generall
and [Councill] at Surat dated 25th January last and a General [from] the Agent
&c. in Persia dated 15th October 1703.

Dispatched ⅌ Pattamar [a Gen^ll. Letter to] Mr. William Tillard at Metchlepatam.

Sloop [Greyhound] Samuel Butcher Master [arrived in this] road from [York] 29TH
Fort, by whom received Dupli[cate] of a Letter [from] the Governor and Council
[there, dated] the 20th. March last.

Ship [Queen, Capt.] Legg Commander arr[ived in this road] from [York] 30
Fort by whom received [the Originall] of that of the 20th. March from the
Governour [and Councill] there.

———

AT A CONSULTATION

Present

THOMAS PITT ESQ^R. PRESIDENT & (GOVERNOUR).

WILLIAM FRASER.	THOMAS (WRIGHT).
THOMAS MARSHALL.	JOHN MEVERELL.
THOMAS FREDERICK.	ROBERT RAWORTH.

[Wee expecting] severall horses from Metchlepatam which [were the] New *Persian*
Companys, and now be [long to the] United [Trade,] the charge of keeping *Horse sold*
which [will be considerable :'tis] thought fitting that some be [sold and] *for P^a. 150.*
Mr. [Addison] offering one hundred and (fifty) [Pagodas] for [a grey horse] that
came by the Phœnix, 'tis agreed he h[as the same] delivered, [Wee finding that] *Necauds*
experiment of making [of raw] silk [to be very] chargeable the success of which *sent to*
[depending intirely upon the] well growing of the [Mulberry trees] and [this *Bengall*
Country] being so excessive despair [and dry [that there] is little probability of *and despare*
effecting the same, 'tis therefore agreed that all the Necauds except two be *making*
return'd to Bengall on the Hugliana Ketch, and that the Paymaster gives them *of silk.*
Batty accordingly] and returne [the account of] what they have received to
Bengall with [them.]

Thomas Pitt Esq. President reads his Mint account of the month of March
last and payes into the Rt. Honble. United [Companys Cash] the sume of five
hundred ninety six Pag^s. twenty fanams for custom on Gold coined in the Mint.

Ponagettee Narso &c. Tobacco and Beetle farmers pays into the Rt. Honble.
United Companys Cash the sume of Four hundred thirty three pagodas twelve
famams.

————*FORT ST. GEORGE, MAY 1704*————

The following Generall letters were now read, Viz^t.—

  From the Gen^{ll}. and Council at Surat dated 25th Jan. last.

  From the Agent &c. in Persia dated 25th October 1703.

  From the Governor and Council at York Fort dat^d. 20th March.

  From the Deputy Governour &c. at St. David dated 27th Instant.

Mr. Thomas [Wright] late Sea Customer payes into the Rt. Hon. United Companys cash the sume of Two thousand Pagodas on account Sea Customs.

Ordered that Bastian Carvalle and Augustine de Rozira Topasses be entertained souldiers in this Garrison.

Ordered that the warehousekeeper, paymaster, and storekeeper etc. do each in their employes get ready to send by ship Queen to Bencoolen what stores they have wrote for.

Upon reading of the Letter from the West Coast we were not so much surpriz'd at the strange allteration in their style of what it was formerly, nor at the many saucy and unmannerly expressions and reflections therein, but at their drawing such a [prodigious number of Bills] upon the Governour and [Councill here] amounting to no less than Dollars. 56,782-2-1 [without advising] their necessity for the same [or whether it is for excount] of the United Trade [or the] Separate [Affairs of the Old] Company. There was severall of the [aforesaid Bills] this day presented for acceptance, but [there being so] many reasons appearing at present [against the] paying of them. It is resolved that the far[ther considera]tion and resolution on this weighty affair [be deferr'd] to our next meeting. 'Tis to be observed that [those Inde]pendent gentlemen at the West Coast [did not intend] only to strip us of near all the stock the [Honble. Managers] were pleased to send to this Place, but sent us also an empty ship to provide for without giving us the least [assistance by] loading any Pepper upon her [pretending] [that 'twas the] Hon. Mann[agers] orders that no Pepper should be sent from thence [to this Coast] not as much as upon their own [shipping], there being no voyage presenting for ship Queen, [so as to defray] her demorage, 'tis resolved that she be for[thwith] despatched to the West Coast with one Hundred [tons of] salt Petre and one hundred tons red[wood] [and the Warehousekeeper] is hereby ordered to forthwith load the same And Capt. Legg was now sent for and acquainted with the aforesaid Resolution.

THO. PITT.

WILL: FRASER.

THO:. WRIGHT.

THOM^s. MARSHALL.

JOHN MEVERELL.

THO^s. FREDERICK.

ROB^T. RAWORTH.

Dispatch'd ⅌ Pattamar a Generall Letter to the Deputy Governour and Council of Fort S^t. David for the United Affairs dated this day.

Ship Happyness Capt. Sands Comander arrived in this road from Surat, by whom received the following Letters from the Generall and Council there Viz^t. One Dated the 27th. March last, and one 21st. Ditto. with Copy of three Letters from Capt. William Morrice &c^a. English captives at Muskat, representing the miserable condition they are in.

This evening the Governour had word brought him, y^t. there was the Corps of a White man drove ashore, near Tandore, to which he sent the Doctor to view it, who returned and acquainted him that it had some time lain in the sea, and so disfigured that there was no knowing it, when People were sent to bury it.

  Ketch Josiah sailed out of this road for [Arracan].

  Commence Briggantine arrived in this road from Anjengo.

  Ship Restoration Capt. Perring Commander [arrived in] this road from Goa.

  Sloop Bone Adventure arrived in this r[oad] [from ditto].

——*FORT ST. GEORGE, MAY 1704*——

AT A CONSULTATION

Present

THOMAS PITT ESQ^R. PRESIDENT [& GOVERN^R.]
WILLIAM FRASER.   THOMAS WRIGHT.
THOMAS MARSHALL.   JOHN MEVERELL.
THOMAS FREDERICK.   ROB^T. RAWORTH.

Thomas Pitt Esqr. President reads his Ac[count of the] R^t. Honble. United Companys Cash for the mo[nth of April] last Ballance Pagod^a. 29,563. 34. 1.

Cash Account read for the month of April.

M^r. William Fraser Warehousekeeper [reads his Ware]house Account for the month of March last [and pays] into the R^t. Honble. United Companys Cash [the sum] of Nine Hundred twenty five Pagodas [twenty seven] fanams thirty five Cash as the Ballance of his Account Goods sold.

Warehousekeepers Account for March read & Pa. 925 : 27. 35. p^d. into Cash.

The Governour being acquainted that the Buxee was set out of S^t. Thoma towards [the Mount] in order to go to the Camp, he yesterday [morning sent] Narrain with the One Hundred Pag^a. Gold Chains [agreed to be sent] him which he kind[ly] received [assuring] he would on all occasions be a freind to the Comp^s. affaires M^r. John Meverell Late Land Customer reads his Land Custom Account for the month of March last. Viz^t.

[Pags.] 100 of Gold chains Presentd [the] Buxee.

Choultry Custom	...	...	...	...	Pag^a. 321 : 25 : 56
Rubie Broakers	...	...	...	...	52 : 26 : 62
Town Broakers	...	...	...	...	2 : 26 : 53
Registring Slaves	...	...	...	...	— : 32 : —

Pag^a. 378 : 3 : 11

and payes into the R^t. Honble. United Companys Cash six hundred Pagod^a. five fanams and Fifteen Cash as the Ballance of his Land Customers Account.

Pag. 600. 5. 15. [paid into] cash, Genl. Letters read.

The following Generalls were read Viz^t. from the Gen^{ll}. and Council at Surat dated 21st March, and from Dittos dated 27th Ditto from Vizagapatam dated 17th April 1704.

There being Two hundred Pagodas offered for the dark grey horse which came from Persia on ship Colchester agreed the same be sold, for the reasons given in our Consultations of the primo Instant.

Ordered that the Storekeeper buys what Timbers is lately come from Pegue, there being a great occasion for them in this Garrison.

Agreed that Twenty five Pag^a. twenty fanams be paid out of Cash for Salary due to M^r. Thomas Matthews deceased.

Agreed that One Thousand Pagod^a. be paid Mr. John Meverell Paymaster to defray Charges Garrison.

M^r. Peter Wallis does now deliver the Ring sent from the West Coast, which is given to M^r. Meverell to make up.

After reading the West Coast [Letter paragraph by] paragraph and likewise what re[lates to that place, wrote] us by the Honble. Mannagers by [the Tavistock and by] the Governour Deputy and Comittees for the [Separate] Affaires of the Old East India Company [to their President] and Council, we Entered upon the {debate whether] we could accept of these Bills drawn on the Go[vernour and Council] of this Place, signed, Richard Watts, [George Shaw and] Charles Wheeler, and after mature consid[eration] thereof concluded that we could not accept the [same for the] following Reasons.

——*FORT ST. GEORGE,. MAY 1704*——

1ˢᵗ. That the Honᵇˡᵉ. Mannagers having made [the place In]dependant
from this, and taken it as they [say themselves] under their immediat Direction
and management [wee] conceive we have no farther to do with them [then as
they] have directed us, which is to furnish them [with what we] find necessary,
particularly a sloop or [Two] of about Thirty Tons, from which we cant inferr
[that they mean] any otherwayes then stores, and not any [money or] the paying
what Bills they shall be pleased [to charge] upon us.

2ᵈˡʸ. That neither by their Letter nor their Bills [do they] distinguish
whose Account it is for, whether [the Account] of the United Trade, or the
Seperate Affaires [of the Old] East India Company, nor as much as pa[rticularize
the] necessity they were under for drawing [such Bills].

3ᵈˡʸ. In the 5ᵗʰ. Paragraph of their Letter [to us they say] the Court of
Mannagers have ordered them to apply themselves to us, to supply their wants of
what properly procureable on this Coast, by which 'tis most undoubtedly mean't
stores and necessaryes and not money.

4ᵗʰˡʸ. That in their Lettter they do not so much as Hint that they have any
orders from the Honᵇˡᵉ. Mannagers to draw Bills on us, for certainly if they had,
they would have remitted us that clause, or a Copy of the whole Letter, if not
thought a lessening to his Honour and Worship Messʳˢ. Watts and Shaw, who
are the Rulers of the rost there, and sole contrivers of the mischievious mannagement that has of late attended the Companys affaires in those parts.

5ᵗʰˡʸ. It can't be immagined that any of these Bills can be for Account of the
Old Company for since July 1702 we have paid West Coast Bills Amounting to
26,000 [lacuna] and remmitted them in stores, and Goods to the Amount of
7057 [lacuna] besides the Old Company who admire to hear that they are in
arrears at the West Coast have ordered in their Letter by the Tavestock if any
thing due there upon their Account, it should be returned them in Goods from
this Place, and not a word mentioned that they have given leave to draw Bills
upon their President and Council here.

6ᵗʰˡʸ. We are of opinion that the Amount of these Bills is not really nor bona-
fide paid into the Companys Cash, but most part of it if not all is for Goods
[delivered] to Messʳˢ. Watts and Shaw, if so, however dispo[s'd of to] workemen or
Merchants the Profit thereof [ought to be] brought to the Companys Account the
truth [of which] we are so well satisfied in, that had not the [Company] cutt off
their subordination, we would have [sent] hence Commissioners to examine into
this [and other] miscarriages; which should have done the [Company] Justice
therein.

7ᵗʰˡʸ. To have paid these Bills would have [rendered us] uncapable to make
any Investment for yᵉ [Tavistock] or Provision for the Sidney, all of them
[amounting to] Pagodˢ. 33,401 : 6:, which is more then [we have in] Cash of
both Companys, and for taking [up money at] Interest we have no orders from the
[United Trade] nor have they sent any seal to enable [us thereto]

The refusing payment of these Bills [has occasion'd] no small muttering in
this Place nor can [wee think it] otherwayes then a very great hardship up
[on them the] Persons to whom the money is due, for [whereas from the]
first settlement of the West Coast it has [been] [subordi]nate to this
Presidency and Persons who [traded thither] were requested and
incouraged to give their [Settlements] Credit and take their Bills upon
this Pre[sidency] by whom the Exchange was settled at 17.[Dollers] for 10
Pagodas which liberty of drawing on us has hi[therto been a] practice and may
be justly said the [support of the] Place. We therefore think it our duty and
obligation not onely in regard to Justice but for the support of the Honour of
that Interest for which these Bills hereafter shall appear to be drawn, do declare
and promise that if these Bills are not paid nor satisfyed by the Governour and
Council of York Fort who drew them, that then we the President and Council here

————*FORT ST. GEORGE, MAY 1704*————

think ourselves obliged to pay the same as soon as we shall be enabled thereto
with £ight ℈ Cent Interest from the time of their being due, and in case they
should not be complyed with during the time of the present,President and Council
we then recommend it to those that shall succeed us charging it upon them as a
piece of Justice not to be neglected or deferred, It being well known to multitudes
of People that the practice of drawing Bills on us has gained them the Credit of
these Bills, tho for the present we must declare we can give no future incouragement for accepting West Coast Bills till we receive farther orders from the Honble.
Mannagers.

THo. PITT.
WILL. FRASER.
THO : WRIGHT.
THOM^s. MARSHALL.
JOHN MEVERELL.
THOM^s. FREDERICK.
ROB^r. RAWORTH.

　Commence Briggantine Nicholas Audney Master sail'd out of this road for
Bengall.

　Ship Stretham returned into this road having [beat for a] Passage to　10
Fort S^t. David but[|could get no farther there Covelong the wind and Current
being against [Her].

　Briggantine Destiny M^r. Edward Master sail'[d for] Fort S^t. David.　　　14

　Ship Francis sailed for Vizagapatam.　　　15

AT A CONSULTATION

Present

<table>
<tr><td colspan="2">THOMAS PITT ESQ^R. President & [Govern^r.]</td><td rowspan="3">TUESDAY
16TH.</td></tr>
<tr><td>WILLAM FRASER.</td><td>THOMAS WRIGHT.</td></tr>
<tr><td>THOMAS MARSHALL.</td><td>JOHN MEVERELL.</td></tr>
<tr><td>THOMAS FREDERICK</td><td>ROBERT RAWORTH.</td></tr>
</table>

　M^r. Thomas Wright Late Sea Customer [reads] his Custom Account for
the month of March [last] Viz^t.

	Pa.
Custom on Goods Imported & exported y^s. [month].	2967　0　0
To Custom on Grain　...　　...　　...　　...　　...	[674 19 44]
To Anchorage ...　　...　　...　　...　　...　　...	[53　0　0]
To Freight ℈ Colchester from Bengall [and] Metchle- patam.	[9 13 54]
To the amount of Goods sold out of the Sea Gate Godowns the owners being unknown.	[35 25　0]
To[tal]　...	[3739 22 18]

· and payes into the R^t. Honble. United Com[pany's Cash] [two] thousand Pagod^s.
on that Account.

　M^r. Thomas Marshall Late Paymaster reads his Paymasters Account for the
month of March last Viz^t.

	Pa.
Charges Garrison　　...　　...　　...　　...　　...	1217 : 24 :
Charges Cattle　...　　...　　...　　...　　...　　...	60 :　8 :
Silk Wormes　　...　　...　　...　　...　　...	15 :　1 :
Charges of Dyett and allowances　　...　　...　　...	303 : 27 :

————*FORT ST. GEORGE, MAY 1704*————

							Pa.
Stores	...	...	...	...	...	...	552 : 27 :
Charges Generall	...	...	...	...	...	...	339 : 4 :
Fort Sᵗ. David	...	...	...	...	...	...	7 : 26 :
Pulo Condore	...	...	...	...	...	...	885 : 3 :
Factors Provisions ...	...	...	...	...	...	...	14 : 27 :
Charges Extraordinary	...	...	...	...	...	...	84 : 10 :
Black Stone ...	...	...	...	...	...	...	8 : 27 :
Fortification and repairs	...	...	...	...	...	...	500 : 31 :

Pagˢ. ...   3516 : 23 :

and payes into the Rᵗ. Honᵇˡᵉ. United Companys Cash seaventeen Pagodas and 28 fanams as the Ballance of his Paymasters Accounts.

Mʳ : William Jennings Steward payes into the Rᵗ. Honᵇˡᵉ. United. Companys Cash Two hundred and seaven Pagodˢ. twenty three fanams and sixty Cash for salt Pork sold to Europe Shipping. ✦

Doctʳ. Bulkly payes into the Rᵗ. Honᵇˡᵉ. United Companys Cash Twenty three Pagodˢ. for Physick sold to ship Tavestock, being in great want for the same.

Agreed that One Thousand Pagodˢ. be paid to Mʳ. John Meverell Paymaster for defraying Charges Garrison.

Mʳ : William Warr Publick Notary did now appear before the Governour and Council with the West Coast Bills recᵈ. by ship Queen demanding their acceptance and Payment. 'Twas unanimously [agreed] in the negative, that we would neither accept nor pay them for the following reasons [Vizᵗ. that] the Governour and Council of Bencoolen [who drew] these Bills have not distinguish'd by Letter or the Bills whether they are on Account of the United Trade [or] the Seperate Affaires of the Old East India Com[pany].

2ᵈˡʸ. The Amount of the Bills is more money [than in] Cash of both Companys, whereupon the Pu[blick No]tary brought with him, Mʳ. Coningsby Mʳ. [Benyon] and Mʳ. Friend, and declared the Bills Pro[tested, that] the Persons to whom they were payable [would return] them to the severall Persons that remitted [them hither].

Messʳˢ. Brewster and Daniel Supra [Cargoes of] Ship Stretham delivers in a Paper for [our advice] relateing to their proceeding to Chiua, which [paper and] our answere thereto is as Entered [after this Consulta]tion.

> THO. PITT.
> WILL : FRASER.
> THO : WRIGHT.
> THOMˢ : MARSHALL.
> JOHN MEVERELL.
> THOˢ. FREDERICK.
> ROBᵀ. RAWORTH.

Ship " Sumarteen " sailed for Bengal [Cojati Awannah] Noquidah
Sloop Coda Bux suild for Fort St. David.

To THE HONᵇˡᵉ. THOMAS PITT ESQᴿ.
PRESIDENT OF THE COAST OF CHOROMANDELL, AND
GOVERNOUR OF. FORT Sᵀ. GEORGE &Cᴬ. COUNCIL.

HONᵇˡᵉ. Sᴿ. &Cᴬ.

The great experience your Honour &ca have in the China Trade Induces us to request your advice [in this] affair. Our intentions have hitherto been for A-[moy] but upon farther considerations do propose going to [Canton] The motives that leads us thereto are, the miserable [account] we have from that Place of

————FORT ST. GEORGE, MAY 1704————

the perfidiousness of the [merchants] and the uncertainty of Trade there, confirmed to us by [late] instances not unknown to your Honour &cᵃ. beside the Government having engrossed the Trade in[to their] own hands we must reasonably expect great de[lays] in our business taking at last whatever Comm[odity] they put upon us at their own rates. Whereas [Canton] being a Port more free and open, and the Company ['s in]terest as well as our own Credit requiring expedi[tion] in dispatching our Affaires, which for the foreg[oing] reasons; We humbly beg your opinions here in, which [will] infinitely oblige.

FORT Sᵀ. GEORGE
MAY 11ᵀᴴ. 1704.

Honᵇˡᵉ. Sʳ. &cᵃ
Your most humble Ser[vants]
CHRISTOPHER BREW[STER].
WILLIAM [DANIEL].

To MESSʳˢ. BREWSTER AND DANIEL
[SUPRA] CARGOES OF SHIP STRETHAM.

We received yours of the 11ᵗʰ. Inst[ant] wherein you desire our advice whether you had best [go] to Amoy or Canton, whereto we can returne no [other] answere then to advise you to keep up to the Com[panys] orders, for as you are not in any respect under our[direc]tion so neither do we think it safe for us to ad[vise] as much as the discretionall part; The usage Mʳ. [Dolben] met at Amoy you have had a full Account [thereof] so that upon the whole matter we conclude [with this] that had we a ship of our own to send to China [wee] should think the Port of Canton the most Eligible [for] the very reason you yourselves give in your [Paper] so wish you a good and prosperous Voyage [We are]

FORT Sᵀ. GEORGE
16ᵀᴴ. MAY 1704.

Sʳˢ.
Your Assured Friends [and]
Humble Servants.
THOMAS PITT.
WILLIAM FRASER.
THOMAS WRIGHT.
THOMAS MARSHALL.
JOHN MEVERELL.
THOMAS FREDERICK.
ROBᵀ. RAWORTH.

Sloop Vizagapatam Merchant sailed for Vizagapatam.   17

Ship Stretham Capᵗ. Flint Commandʳ. sailed out of this road for Atcheen and China.   19

Ship Pembrooke Frigat Andrew Gatt Master arrived in this road from Surat by whom received Copy of our last Letter from the Generall and Council there.

Ship Sᵗ. Joan arrived in this road from Surat Co[ja] Michael Noquedah.   22

Received ℔ Pattamars a Generall Letter from Mʳ. Wil[liam] Tillard at Metchlepatam dated 11ᵗʰ. Instant.

AT A CONSULTATION

Present

[TUESDAY
23D.]

THOMAS PITT ESQ^R. President and Gov[ernour.]
    WILLIAM FRASER.   THOMAS WRIGHT.
    THOMAS MARSHALL.   JOHN MEVERELL.
    THOMAS FREDERICK.   ROBERT RAWORTH.

Land
Customer's.
Acco^t. read.

M^r. Thomas Frederick Land Customer reads his Land Custom Account for the month of April last Viz^t.

To Choultry Custom ...	...	...	...	Pa. 504: 6:14
Rubie Broakers ...	...	...	...	43: 6:73
Town Broakers ...	...	...	...	3:27:15
Registring Slaves ...	...	...	...	:32:
			Pag^s:	552: 0:22

Pag^s. [543:
22: 22 paid]
into cash.

and payes into the R^t. Honble. United Companys Cash[five] hundred forty three Pagod^s. twenty two fanams and twenty two Cash.

[Payment]on
Acco^t. Sea
Customs.

M^r. Thomas Wright Late Sea Customer payes into the R^t. Honble. United Companys Cash One Thousand Pags on Account Sea Customs.

1000 pags.
repaid into
Cash [for]
Town Wall.

M^r. Thomas Marshall Late Paymaster payes into [the] R^t. Honble. United Companys Cash the sume of One Thousand Pagodas, being money he received Account building the Black Town Wall and Workes.

[P^s. 1000]p^d.
towards
building
[the] Black
Town Wall.

Agreed that One Thousand Pagodas be paid M^r. John Meverell Paymaster towards building the Black Town Wall and workes.

Mint Acco^t.
for April &
Pa 469 : 25
p^d. into
Cash on y^t.
Account.

Thomas Pitt Esqr. as Mintmaster reads his [Mint] Account for the month of April last, and [payes into the R^t Honble. United Companys Cash the sume of [four hundred and] sixty nine Pagod^s. twenty five fan^s. on that [Account].

[Letter]
rec^d. read.

Generall Letter from M^r. William Tillard at Metchlepatam dated 11th. Instant now read.

[P^s. 2] 5 p^d.
Town Coni-
cop[plys]
duty.

Agreed that Twenty five Pagodas be paid [Mananga]pau for Three months Town Conicoplyes Duty [ending] ultimo April 1704.

[Souldier
discharged
[another]
Entertaind.

Ordered that Bastian Lewall at his request [be dis]charged from farther service in this Garrison and Antonio Johanna Topaz be Entertaind in his [room]

[Sebastian]
Rebeira
[pe]titions.

The Petition of Sebastian Rebeira laying claim to the Estate of Pasquall De Grace was now read [which] is referred to the Court of Admiralty to examine into what Alledged therein, and report their opinion [upon] it.

[Hu]glyana
Ketoh or-
[dered] to be
sold at Out-
cry [and] the
Compa. to
buy.

[Salt] to be
sent on
Ketch.

There being a great necessity to send a Vessell [to the] West Coast for their speedy answere relating to the [Bills they] drew on us by the Queen, that so we may pre[vent any in]conveniency that may attend the United Trade [if the amount of the Bills] or any part thereof be for Account [of the old] Company by taking speedy care to pay the same, for [which] reason we have Agreed to send the Huglyana Ketch [thither but she being Invoiced at such an extravagant rate from Bengall, we think it reasonable that she be put up at [out]cry the 25th. Instant and that the Sea Customer buys [her] for Account of the United Trade. Agreed that as soon as the Huglyana Ketch is bought at Outcry that the Warehousekeeper loads on her for the West Coast Forty Tons Salt Petre and twenty Tons redwood.

—————FORT ST, GEORGE, MAY 1704—————

The House commonly called Mʳ. Jearseys House [being] very much out of repair 'tis ordered that the Paymaster forthwith sett people to work to repair it thorowly and [that] Mʳ. Wright who Lodges in it supervise the same.

'Tis Agreed that all the Woolen Manufactury belonging to the United Company be put up to outcry this day of seaven night being 30ᵗʰ. Instant.

Paupiah the Braminy who is our only Linguister [yᵗ.] Translates Persians, Gentues &cᵃ. delivered in a Petition to have his Pay advanced from Five to eight Pagodas a month, which we think very reasonable considering the service he do's, and accordingly the Paymaster is to pay him eight Pagodᵃ. a month to commence from the first of next month.

Mr. Jearseys house to be repaired.

Woollen Manufactory to be sold.

[Paupiah Braminy wages advanced to] pag. 8 per mensem.

THO. PITT.
WILL. FRASER.
THO. WRIGHT.
THOMˢ. MARSHALL.
JOHN MEVERELL.
THOMˢ. FREDERICK.
ROBᵀ. RAWORTH.

Ship Gralvis arrived in this road from Trincombar⸴   24

This Day the Governor recᵈ. advices from Pollicat that Monhʳ. Johannes Slyland lately Chief for the D[utch] Affairs at Metchlepatam was arrived there [in order] to his going to Negapatam to take charge of the Government and Directore on the Coast.   25

This day arrived the Metchlepatam Horses, one [being] left on the road, which was not able to come [thorow]..   28

AT A CONSULTATION

Present

MONDAY 29ᵀᴴ

THOMAS PITT ESQᴿ. President & [Govʳ.]
WILLIAM FRASER.   THOMAS WRIGHT.
THOMAS MARSHALL.   JOHN MEVERELL.
THOMAS FREDERICK   ROBᵀ. RAWORTH.

Tomorrow being the day appointed to sell the Woollen Manufactury, agreed that they be not sold under the following Prizes Vizᵗ.

Aurora at 24 Pagᵃ. ℔ peice   ...   .
Scarlet at 45   Ditto.   ...
Red & Green at 15 Ditto.   ...   .

and to be declared at the sale that the Rᵗ. Honᵇˡᵉ. Company will not make another sale till [Primo] Oc[tober] next.

Generall Letter to the Governour and Council of Bencoolen, to the United Council in the Bay of Bengall [both] dated the 27ᵗʰ. Instant now read and approved.

Agreed that One Thousand Pagodˢ. be paid Mʳ. John Meverell Paymaster for defraying Charges Garrison.

Mʳ. Joseph Hiller Late Provisionall Storekeeper pays into the Rᵗ. Honᵇˡᵉ. United Companys Cash Three Hundred Pagodˢ. on Account Stores sold. ..

————*FORT ST. GEORGE, MAY 1704*————

Ponagettee Narso &cᵃ. Tobacco and Beetle farmers payes into the Rᵗ. Honᵇˡᵉ· United Companys Cash Five Hundred eighty three Pagodˢ. twelve fanˢ. on that Accoᵗ.

THO. PITT.   :
WILL. FRASER.
THO. WRIGHT.   .
THOMˢ. MARSHALL.
JOHN MEVERELL.
THOˢ. FREDERICK.
ROBᵀ. RAWORTH.

31   Received this day ⅌ Pattamar, the following Packets vizᵗ.

From the Chief &. Council of Vizagapatam dated 10ᵗʰ. May [for] the United Affaires.

From Ditto dated 10ᵗʰ. May for the Separate Affairs.

From the Deputy Governour and Council of Fort Sᵗ. David dated 27ᵗʰ. Instant for the United Affaires.

————————————

AT A CONSULTATION

Present

WEDNES-   THOMAS PITT ESQᵃ. President & Governᵣ.
DAY 31ˢᵗ   WILLIAM FRASER.   THOMAS WRIGHT.
               THOMAS MARSHALL.   JOHN MEVERELL.
               THOMAS FREDERICK.   ROBERT RAWORTH.

A Petition of Nalla Mutty Relick of [Wallaca] Chittee Deceased concerning the Estate of [Her deceased Hus]band in the Hands of Chinandee Chittee [was now read.] Tis agreed that [the] Examination of what [alledg'd in] the Petition be [refe]rred to six of the Casts and that the Braminy Paupiah brings in a List of the Heads of the Casts to the Governour and Council, out [of] which the same to be chosen and they to make their [report to the] Board.

Mᵣ. John Meverell Paymaster reads his [Paymaster's] Account for the month of April last, Vizᵗ.

					Pagˢ.
Charges Garrison	...	...	...	...	...1488 : [14
Charges Cattle	...	...	...	...	... 69 : [9
Silk Wormes	...	...	...	...	... 14 : [5 . . .
Charges Dyet and allowances		...	...	...	... 289 : [17 . .]
Stores	...	...	...	...	... 42 : [12 . .]
Charges Generall	...	...	...	...	... 378 : [21 . .]
Charges Extraordinary	...	...	...	...	... 13 : [10 . .]
Pulo Condore	...	...	...	...	...106 : [15 . .]
Black Stone .	...	...	...	...	... 9 : [— . .]
Fortification and repairs	...	...	...	...	... 151 : [34 . .]

Pagˢ. ... 2262 : [29 . .].

The following Generall Letters were now read Vizᵗ.
From Vizagapatam dated 10ᵗʰ. May 1704.

————*FORT ST. GEORGE, JUNE 1704*————

From Fort S^t. David dated 27th. Instant, as also a Letter to the Deputy Governour and Council of Fort S^t. David dated this day now read and approved.

> THO: PITT.
> WILL: FRASER.
> THO: WRIGHT.
> THOM^s: MARSHALL.
> JOHN: MEVERELL.
> THOM^s: FREDERICK.
> ROB^r: RAWORTH.

Dispatchd ℞ Pattamars two Packets for Fort S^t. David for the Seperate and United Affaires both dated yesterday. JUNE ℞^{mo}.

Ship Madapollam Laulchad Noquedah saild for [Arracan]. 2

Ship Restoraton Capt. Perring Comander sail'd out of [this] road for Bengall by whom sent two Packets both dated the 27th Instant for the United and Separate Affsirs. 3

Sloop Bone Adventure sailed for Bengall Sam^{ll}. Bowcher [Master]
Ship Happyness sailed for Bengall Capt. Sands Com[and^r.]
Ship Sedgwick Capt. Rawlings Com^r. sailed for Bengall.
Ship Gralvis sailed for Bengall.
Ship Seermary arrived in this road from Surat Coja [Auga]nure Noquedah. 8

Ship Humphrey and Charles Capt. Wright Com^r. arrived in this road from Gombroone in Persia, by whom received a Generall Letter from the Chief and Council there dated 28th. April last.

Ship Sta. Cruce sailed out of this Road to the southward,

Received ℞ Pattamars a Generall Letter from the Deputy Governour and Council of Fort S^t. David dated 10th. [Instant] with Copy of their Diary and Consultations to the [26th May 1704.] 13

———

AT A CONSULTATION

Present

THOMAS PITT ESQ^R. President & Governour.
WILLIAM FRASER.　　THOMAS WRIGHT.
THOMAS MARSHALL.　JOHN MEVERELL.
THOMAS FREDERICK.　ROBERT RAWORTH.

Thomas Pitt Esqr. President reads his [account of] the R^t. Honble. United Companys Cash for the m[onth of] May last Ballance Pagod^s. 36239 : 29 : 5.

Generall Letter from the Chief and Council [of Gombroon] dated 28th. April last, and from the Deputy Gov[ernour and] Council of Fort S^t. David dated 10th. Instant [both now read].

Agreed that One Thousand Pagodas be [paid] Mr. John Meverell Paymaster to defray Charges [Garrison.]

M^r. Thomas Marshall Sea Customer payes into the R^t. Honble. United Companys Cash the sume [of] one Thousand Pagod^s. on account Sea Customs.

M^r. Peter de Pomera &c^a. Arrao Farmers payes in [to] the R^t. Honble. United Companys Cash the sume of Five Hundred fifty four Pagod^s. sixteen fanams in part of the Debt owing to the R^t. Honble. Company by Gruapau &c^a. old Tobacco Farmers.

————FORT ST. GEORGE, JUNE 1704————

    Ordered that the Warehousekeeper buys one Thousand Candy of Redwood to lye by for a store, and that he advances money for the same as he sees occasion.

    This day in Consultation Mr. Dolben made a Proposall to us of Freighting the ship Queen for China (w[hich] we were just Dispatching for the West Coast) which [we] were willing to hearken thereto by reason that the Governour and Council there were very doubtfull whether they shall be able to load Her for England, and de[sire] us to Employ her if possible, so that 'twas Agreed [that] the following demands be made if they Freighted the aforesaid Ship to China. The Freighters either to pay the Companys Demorage during the time of the Voyage or Five Thousand five Hundred Pagodas, and that they shall be obliged to Dispatch her from China to this Port by the Tenth of December, and whereas he did likewise propose that she might goe from China to Persia or that if she arrived so early here as to save her Passage thither that she might proceed on that Voyage from hence for which Voyage it was Agreed to Lett her for Eight Thousand five Hundred Pagodas, and the Secretary to acquaint Mr. Dolben [with] the same.

Tho. Pitt.
Will. Fraser.
Tho. Wright.
Thoˢ. Marshall.
John Meverell.
Thoˢ. Frederick.
Robᵗ. Raworth.

16   Dispatchd ⅌ Pattamars a Generall Letter to Mr. William Tillard at Metchlepatam dated yesterday.

AT A CONSULTATION

Present

THURSDAY   THOMAS PITT Esqʳ. President & Govʳ.
15ᵀᴴ.   WILLIAM FRASER.   THOMAS WRIGHT.
             THOMAS MARSHALL.   JOHN MEVERELL.
             THOMAS FREDERICK.   ROBERT RAWORTH.

    Mr. Dolben was this day again in Consultation who acquainted us he had conferred with the Persons that were to be concerned in Freighting Ship Queen for China and Persia, who in consideration of the dearness of [silver, as also] the small quantity procureable, and the ill[treatment] they must expect in China in buying of their [goods,] they had come to this result, that unless we would Let them the Ship for Eight Thousand Pagodas to China and Persia they would desist from thinking any more of this matter which we told him we would consider of and return our speedy answere. So after having Debated this amongst ourselves, and all of us inferring from the West Coast Letters that they would not be able to dispatch her for England whereby her demorage would be a heavy Loss to yᵉ. Company besides her Men being in no good state of health would [not] a little indanger their lives, and so consequently the ruin of the ship, which induced us to conclude to Lett [the] ship to Freight for China and Persia at Eight Thousand Pagodas to be paid on her returno from Persia to this Port and that the Freighters have the whole ship, reserving [the] Priviledges to the ships Company, and that there be noe manner of Disputes on her returne whether she carrys her Tonnage or No, 'Tis likewise agreed that the ship brings freight free from Persia for the Company One Hundred Chests of Wine, Rosewater and Fruit, and six Persia horses if the Companys Chief there shall put them on board.

———*FORT ST. GEORGE, JUNE 1704*———

Ordered that the Warehousekeeper do's forthwith unload all the Redwood and Salt Petre &cᵃ. Loaden on board ship Queen for the West Coast also send for ashore the redwood out of the Hughly[anah] [Ketch and order all] the stores intended for the [West Coast to be travers'd on] board the Ketch, and that Mʳ. Edward Jones [be sent] off to do the same.

> Tʜᴏ. Pɪᴛᴛ.
> Wɪʟʟ. Fʀᴀsᴇʀ.
> Tʜᴏ. Wʀɪɢʜᴛ.
> Tʜᴏmˢ. Mᴀʀsʜᴀʟʟ.
> Jᴏʜɴ Mᴇᴠᴇʀᴇʟʟ.
> Tʜᴏmˢ. Fʀᴇᴅᴇʀɪᴄᴋ.
> Roʙᴛ. Rᴀᴡᴏʀᴛʜ.

Aᴛ ᴀ Coɴsᴜʟᴛᴀᴛɪᴏɴ

Present

. Tʜᴏᴍᴀs Pɪᴛᴛ Esqᴿ. Pʀᴇsɪᴅᴇɴᴛ ᴀɴᴅ Gᴏᴠᴇʀɴᴏᴜʀ.

Wɪʟʟɪᴀᴍ Fʀᴀsᴇʀ.	Tʜᴏᴍᴀs Wʀɪɢʜᴛ.
Tʜᴏᴍᴀs Mᴀʀsʜᴀʟʟ.	Jᴏʜɴ Mᴇᴠᴇʀᴇʟʟ.
Tʜᴏᴍᴀs Fʀᴇᴅᴇʀɪᴄᴋ.	Roʙᴇʀᴛ Rᴀᴡᴏʀᴛʜ.

Thomas Pitt Esqʳ. as Mintmaster reads his M[int Accᵗ.] for the month of May last, and payes into the Right Honᵇˡᵉ. United Companys Cash Three hundred twenty [two Pagodas] fifteen fanamas sixty Cash as the Ballance of that month's Account.

Mʳ. Robert Raworth Storekeeper reads his [Storekeeper's] Account for the month of May last.

Mʳ. Thomas Frederick Land Customer reads his Land Custom Account for the month of May last Vizᵗ.

To Choultry Custom	... ...	Pagˢ.	415 : 32 : 65
To Rubie broakers	... ...		69 : 2 : 65
To Town broakers	... ...		9 : 6 : 73
Registring slaves	... ...		... 32 : ...
		Pagˢ.	495 : 2 : 43

Mʳ. Thomas Marshall Sea Customer reads his Sea Custom Account for the month of April last.

Custom on Goods Imported & exported this Moᵗʰ.	... ...	Pa.	2,341 : 13 : 44
Custom on Grain	... ...		386 : 6 : 16
Anchorage	... ...		53 : 18 : —
		Pa.	2,781 : 1 : 60

and payes into the Rᵗ. Honᵇˡᵉ. United Companys Cash the sume of One Thousand Pagodas on that Account.

Mʳ. Thomas Marshall Late Paymaster reads [his] Account Disbursements of the Black Town Wall and Works and payes into the Rᵗ. Honᵇˡᵉ. United Companys Cash the sum of Two hundred thirty nine Pagodˢ. twenty eight fanams sixteen Cash, as the Ballance of that Account.

Agreed that one Thousand Pagodas be paid to Mʳ. John Meverell Paymaster to defray Charges Garrison.

Capᵗ. William Legg Commander of Ship Queen delivers in a request for the Payment of what money allowed him by Charterparty to be taken up in India being Nine hundred and sixty Dollars, which is agreed to be paid him and his request is as Enterd after this Consultation.

g

——FORT ST. GEORGE, JUNE 1704——

The President produces a Letter he received [from] [Dowed] Cawn wherein he desires Liquors, which is agreed to be sent him.

The President acquainted the Council that [Senr.] Gregoria Parran had been with him this morning [who] told him he had a message from the Phousdar of [S^t. Thoma] desiring that the Governour would permit him to come to this Town to discourse with him about the [business] of Coja Awan and Coja Timore being very desir[ous to] propose meanes to accommodate that matter, s[o as to] preserve his Friendship with this Place,' Tis [agreed that] he be permitted to come.

In the Year 1702 when Dowed Cawn was besieging this Place, the Governour sent the Bedford sloop [to] Trincombar for Provisions, but meeting with a long passage was streightend for water so that they [archor'd] at [*lacuna*] in the King of Tanjores Country [where] the People seiz'd the Vessell and all the men [and put them] in Prison, where they lay severall months and were us'd barbarously, the Vessell they hawl'd into a [small river] and tooke out her Guns which were four and [also ten] Candy of China root and sent it to the King [Upon this] the President wrote severall Letters to his [Chief Ministers] demanding satisfaction but all the answer [could be] had they pleaded the Vessell was a wreck [and so of course] their right, at which time the Merchants [of Tanjore] had severall effects here, which the President [would have] seized, but that a Merchant here one Sunca[Rama] who has great dealings at Tanjore pretended that he would accommodate the matter and procure satisf[action. but] not having hitherto done Any thing in it, [The President] acquainted the Council that he had few dayes past seiz'd Goods that came from Tanjore for satisfaction for the aforesaid vessell and Cargoe, unto which the Council unanimously assented, hoping thereby to discourage those Country People and those adjacent to us from doing the like.

Kittee Narrain with whom severall English were concerned sent likewise a Boat near Two yeares since to the southward into Mangamaus Country where the Chief Minister seizd and tooke from their Conicoply upwards of One Thousand Pagodas, and there being lately some of that Ministers Goods arrived here, Agreed that the same be stop'd till satisfaction be made.

THO. PITT.
WILL FRASER.
THO WRIGHT.
THOM^s. MARSHALL.
JOHN MEVERELL.
THOM^s. FREDERICK.
ROB^T. RAWORTH.

To [THE H]ON^BLE. THOMAS PITT. ESQ^R.
[PRESI]DENT AND GOVERN^R. OF
[FORT ST.] GEORGE &C^A. COUNCIL.

S .

Having occasion for money for the Service of Ship Queen, and it being agreed in Charterparty made between the Honble. Mannagers for the United Trade and the Owners of said ship that Dollars [Nine] hundred and sixty shall be paid the Comander [in India] for that purpose if required, I therefore re[quest] Your Hon^r. and Council will please to order the same to be pay'd.

S^rs.

FORT S^T. GEORGE
22^d. June 1704.

Your most [Humble] Servant
W[ILLIAM LEGG]

AT A CONSULTATION

Present

THOMAS PITT ESQ^R. PRESIDENT AND GOVERN^R.
WILLIAM FRASER   THOMAS WRIGHT.
THOMAS MARSHALL.   JOHN MEVERELL.
THOMAS FREDERICK.   ROBERT RAWORTH.

Generall Letter from the Deputy Governour and Council of Fort S^t. David dated 21st. Instant now read.

M^r. Thomas Marshall payes into the Right Honble. United Companys Cash the sume of Eighty one Pagodas, one fanam, being part of what he paid as the [bal]lance of his Paymasters Account 13th. May 1703, but the President Debted the Cash short that [sum which] is now cleared by paying the same.

M^r. Thomas Marshall Sea Customer re[ads his Sea Cus]tom Account for May last Viz^t.

To Custom on Goods Imported & exported this
    month ...   .   P. 2312. 30. 22
To Custom on Grain 687. 30. 76
To Anchorage   ...   .   50. 18. —
                                              3051. 7. 18

M^r. Thomas Marshall delivers in [a Petition des]iring leave to lay down the Companys ser[vice in] order to proceed on a Voyage to China, which is accordingly granted, and his Petition Ent^d. after this Consultation.

M^r. Thomas Marshall Judge Advocate produces an Account of what money now lyes in Court, which is ordered to be paid into the R^t. Honble. United Companys Cash being Nine Thousand Seaven hundred seaventy five Pagodas and thirty Fanams, the particulars of which is as followes Viz^t.

To Nina Chittee Ballance redwood   ... Pa.   2 : 1 : 50
To M^r. Soames   ⎫   36 : 35 : 31
To M^r. Warren   ⎪ Acco^t. M^r. Halls   62 : 7 : 68
To M^r. White   ⎬   dividend   ...   156 : 26 : 55
To Capt. Adams ⎭   73 : 35 : 15
To Coja Awan Attatch'd by the Attorneys
    of Coja Usuph ...   .   6845 : 18 : —
To Pasquall De Grasse Estate   ...   ...   2598. 13 : 21
                               Pag^s. 9775 : 30 : —

- Articles of Agreement between the President & Council and the Freighters of Ship Queen were now read, and agreed upon ; ordered to be drawn out fair to be signed and Entered after this Consultation.

Ordered that Mark Rayes and Antony Merino be Entertain'd Souldiers in this Garrison and that John Phillips one of the Gunners Crew at his request be discharged.

Ordered that the Paymaster muster Queen's ship's Company and report the same to this Board.

By M^r. Marshall's laying down the service [the Sea] Customer and Judge Advocates Places are vacant and considering the season of the year we [have] just reason to expect ships from Europe very [suddenly] when it may happen the Company may think fitt to make [al]terations in their Council upon which 'tis [agreed that] no removall be made for the present [But whereas] M^r. Wright the Warehousekeeper has [no extraordi]nary business upon his Hands at this time ['tis order'd] that he supplyes the Place of Sea Custom[er till the] arrivall of the shipping or that the President [and Councill] shall direct otherwayes

————*FORT ST. GEORGE, JUNE 1704*————

therein, and 'tis [likewise agreed] that the Judge Advocates Place be vacant [till the] arrivall of the shipping, or that the President [and Councill] shall find it necessary to fill the same.

> Thomas Pitt.
> Will: Fraser.
> Tho: Wright.
> Thom⁸. Marshall.
> John Meverell.
> Thom⁸. Frederick.
> Rob⁷. Raworth.

To The Hon'ble Thomas Pitt, Esq.
      President and Governour of
         Fort St. George &c⁴. Council.

Honble. S^r. &c^a.

Your Honour &c^a. are not insensible of my intentions of returning shortly for England, and my desire of seeing something more of this part of the world then I have yet done, by which I may likewise render myself more capable of serving the Hon'ble Company as well in other parts of the world as here, which I shall be ready to do on all occasions.

The present opportunity of seeing China makes me renew my request of leaving their Hon^rs. service, but not without some regret, having received many favours from them, and shall embrace all opportunityes to make my due acknowledgement of the same, I beg you'l be pleased to grant me my request which will add to the obligations of·

> · Honble. S^r. &c^a.
> Your obed^t. Humble Servant,

Fort St. George,
26th June 1704.   ·Thòmas Marshall.

Contract and Agreement, by and [between]· the Hon'ble President and Council of Fort St. George for Account of the Rt. Honble. United English East India Company and [John] Dolben Esq. &c. Freighters of Ship Queen burthen [three] hundred and twenty tons or thereabouts, William Legg Commander, now riding in the [Road] of Madras [accord^g.] to Charterparty made between the Rt. Honble. United English East India Company and her owners in England dated the 23rd day of December.1702 which said Charterparty with and every its Tonnage, Priviledges [under] obligations we the said President and Council do assign and make over unto the said John [Dolben] Esq. [&ca.] Freighters to have the sole Lading [and] Freightment thereof to the Port of Canton or any [other port in China] and so hither again and to [Gombroone in Persia] or from Malacca to Persia directly and hither again if the Supra Cargoes of said ship [shall think] [con]venient for the consideration and [sum of eight] Thousand Pagodas Currant of Madrass [to be payable] the said John Dolhon Esqr. &ca. Freight[ers] executors, administrators and assigns [into the said] President and Council or their successors [within thirty] dayes after the next arrivall of the said [ship from Gombroone in] Persia to this Port, without any abatement or [deduction] for allowances of short tunnage. Tis also agreed that the said Freighters are [and shall be] at all charges of measuring, Presents; [and other Inci]dents to [Trade] that shall be demanded or may happen during the said Voyage and that she be dispatch'd from China so early as to gain her Passage to Gombroone in Persia and arrive here by the 15th. day of August One Thousand seaven Hundred and Five; and if she stays longer the said Freighters allowing and paying her Charterparty

——FORT ST. GEORGE, JUNE 1704——

Demorage for so many dayes as she arrives after the said 15th. day of August 1705. And it is farther Agreed that in case the said ship shall proceed directly for Persia from China without touching att Fort S^t. George that then it may be Lawfull for the Supra Cargoes to Lade on board any of the Companys ships which they shall meet in China, or Malacca or elsewhere bound to Fort S^t. George, such quantity of Gold as they shall think fit, being part of the stock Laden by the said John Dolben Esqr., &c^a. on said ship to be brought to Fort S^t. George and there delivered to the said John Dolben Esqr. &c^a. without paying any freight for the same, and it is farther agreed by and between the President and Council and y^e. Freighters of the aforesaid ship that they bring Freight free from Persia for Account of the R^t. Honble. United English East India Company One Hundred Chests of Wine, Rosewater and fruit and six Persia Horses if the Comp^s. Chief there shall put them on board. In WITNESS whereof we the President and Council for Account and in behalf of the R^t. Honble. United English East India Company do hereby oblige ourselves on the one part, and John Dolben Esqr. for himself and in behalfe of the Freighters of said ship, on the other part, having hereunto interchangeably set our hands and seals in Fort S^t. George in the City of Madrass this 27th day of June 1704.

JOHN DOLBEN.

Locus Sigili.

[Wit]nesses.
[Gul]ston Addison
[Jose]ph Lister
[Henry] Davenport *Sec^{ry}*.

AT A CONSULTATION

Present

THOMAS PITT ESQ^r. PRESIDENT & GOV[ERNOUR].
WILLIAM FRASER.   THOMAS WRIGHT.
JOHN MEVERELL.   THOMAS FREDERICK.
ROBERT RAWORTH.

The following Generall Letters were now read & sign'd.
To the Governour and Council of Pollicondore.
To the Supra Cargoes of ship Sidney.
To the Supra Cargoes or Commanders of any of the [Company's] ships all dated yesterday as also a Generall to M^r. Tillard dated this day.

Agreed that One Thousand Pagod^s. be paid M^r. John Meverell Paymaster to defray Charges Garrison.

The Contract for freighting ship Queen for China [and] Persia was now interchangeably signed between the President and Council, and M^r. Dolben &c^a. in behalf of the Freighters.

M^{rs}. Eyton widdow of Nathaniel Eyton who lately dyed at Bentall on the West Coast, delivered in a Petition requesting that we would write to the Governor and Council of Bencoolen to appoint someb[ody] to adjust her Husbands Accounts, and after his Debts paid, pay the remainder into the Companys Cash and remitt it hither by Bill for her subsistance.

THO. PITT.
WILL : FRASER.
THO : WRIGHT.
JOHN MEVERELL.
THO^s. FREDERICK.
ROB^t. RAWORTH.

————*FORT ST. GEORGE, JUNE 1704*————

AT A CONSULTATION

Present

THOMAS PITT ESQ^r. PRESIDENT & GOVERN^R.
WILLIAM FRASER.   THOMAS WRIGHT.
JOHN MEVERELL.   THOMAS FREDERICK.
ROBERT RAWORTH.

WEDNES-
DAY 24TH.

Papers delivered in by the Register relating to Coja Timore & Awan.

The Register this day delivered in a parcell of Papers to the Governour and Council sealed up, said to be what Coja Awan delivered to Coja Timore, which was afterwards delivered into the Court and left by the Late Judge Advocate with the Register, which Papers 'tis Agreed they lye in the Cash Chest, till the business between Coja Timore and Coja Awan be ended.

Coja Gregoria &ca. request leave for 37 Bales Goods of Coja Usuph be sent to Manilha.

Coja Gregoria and two Armenians the Attorneys of Coja Usuph setting forth to us that there was thirty seaven Bales of Goods proper for Manilha in the House that Coja Awan lived belonging to Coja Usuph, which they desired they may be permitted to ship on board the Sta. Cruz now bound to Manilha, for whereas they are [dyed] and chay'd Goods, so that lying another year would much impare their Value, which now they esteem to be [upwards] of two Thousand Pagodas.

Agreed the Bales be sent they giving Security.

Tis Agreed that Coja Gregoria and the Two Attorneys have leave to ship off the aforesaid Bales giving [Five] thousand pagodas security to the Governour & Council to indemnify them from any demands that may hereafter be made by Coja Awan.

> THO: PITT.
> WILL: FRASER.
> THO: WRIGHT.
> JOHN MEVERELL.
> THOM^s: FREDERICK.
> ROBT: RAWORTH.

This Morning M^r. Thomas Marshall and M^r. Henry Whistler Supra Cargoes of ship Queen and Capt. William Legg Commander went off on board Ship.

29   About 5 a clock this morning ship Queen sailed out of this road for China.

30   Huglyana Ketch Capt. Hopkins Command^r. sailed out of this road for the West Coast by whom sent a Packet to the Governour and Council of Bencoolen dated 27th. May and 20th. Instant.

Sloop Christian Quintus arrived in this road from Trincombar.

JULY
PMO.

Ship S^t. Joan de Canterbury belonging to the Armenians sailed out of this road for Manilha.

Sloop Christian Quintus sailed for Trincombar.

————

AT A CONSULTATION

Present

THOMAS PITT ESQ^r., PRESIDENT & GOVERN^R.
WILLIAM FRASER.   THOMAS WRIGHT.
JOHN MEVERELL.   THOMAS FREDERICK.
ROBERT RAWORTH.

MONDAY
3d.

[Ps. 1000 advanced] for buying [of] Redwood.

Agreed that One Thousand Pagodas be advanced to M^r. Thomas Wright. Warehousekeeper towards buying of Redwood.

------*FORT ST. GEORGE, JULY 1704*------

Ponagettee Narso &cᵃ. Tobacco and Beetle farmers payes into the Rᵗ. Honᵇˡᵉ. United Companys Cash the sum of Five Hundred eighty three Pagodˢ. and [twelve] fanams on that Account. _583. 12. pd. into Cash by ye. [Tob]acco farmers._

Ordered that the following stores be sent to Fort Sᵗ. David on ship Johanna. Vizᵗ. _[Stores] ordered for Fort St. David._

Kismisses 5 m ᵈ. Raisons 5 mᵈ. Figgs 10 pound Apricocks 10 pound Almonds 4 maund Small Nutts ½ bagg. Pistashes ½ a bagg Prunellaes ½ maund. Wallnutts 200, Syrash wine [10 chests.]

Ordered that John Tandermine and William H[arris] at their request be discharged from farther service in the Gunroome, and that Jacob Stock and Adreon Pe[terson] are Entertained of the Gunroome Crew, and Anto[nio] Rodregues as a souldier in this Garrison. _2 Gunners discharged and 2 souldiers & 2 Gunners Entd._

Ordered that George Ainsworth be Entertained as Cooper in this Garrison, and that the Paymaster payes [him] as such. _Cooper Entertained._

Mʳ. John Meverell Paymaster reads his paymasters Account for the month of May last Vizᵗ. _Paymasters Account read._

					Pa.				
Charges Garrison	...	...	...	...	1159	[10	.	.	]
Charges Cattle ...	...	...	...	...	60:	[28	.	.	]
Silk Wormes	...	...	...	...	12:	[18	.	.	]
Pulo Condore	...	...	...	...	1:	[28	.	.	]
Charges Dett and allowances	...	...	...	267:	[18	40	.	]
Stores	...	...	...	...	113:	[18	40	.	]
Charges Generall	...	...	...	...	319:	[27	.	.	]
Charges Extraordinary	...	...	...	2:	[1:	.	.	]
Fortifications and repairs	...	...	...	69:	[18	.	.	]

$$2006 : [31. =$$

Colloway Chittee and Vinkattee Chittee offering twenty Corge of 40 Covᵈˢ. Betteelaes to sell. 'Tis ordered that they first sort them, and then the Governour and Council will view them and agree [as to] the price thereof. _Betteelas offered to sell._

The two ·aforesaid Persons likewise proposed the furnishing the Company with Long Cloth according as the Mannagers direct, and produced a Muster for _Calloway & Vinkatte offer to contract for both ordrs._

wᶜʰ. they ask'd Thirty two Pagodas ⅌ Corge which we thought not worth more then thirty, of which they were ordered to consider till to morrow, and then give their finall answere. _[Consider]ation deferred till next morning._

> THO. PITT.
> WILL. FRASER.
> THO. WRIGHT.
> JOHN MEVERELL.
> THOˢ. FREDERICK.
> ROBᵀ. RAWORTH.

AT A CONSULTATION

Present

THOMAS PITT ESQ.ᴿ. PRESIDENT AND GOVERNOUR.
WILLIAM FRASER. THOMAS WRIGHT.
JOHN MEVERELL. THOMAS FREDERICK.
ROBERT RAWORTH.

[TUESDAY] 4ᵗʰ.

Wollacca Chittees widdow having formerly complained in a Petition to us, of great Injustices done Her by one Chinandee Chittee, the examination of which _Petition of Wollacca Chittees_

————*FORT ST. GEORGE, JULY 1704*————

widdow referr'd to six of their Casts.

was Agreed in Consultation the 31ˢᵗ May last to be refer[red] to the Cast, and this day a List of some Persons being delivered in, 'Tis ordered that the following Persons do examine the whole matter with all expedition, and make their report to the Governour and Council Viz. Vincattee Yerwallapa Madua, Pegu Nulla Sanady, Vincatte Puttee, Colloway Chittee.

Diana Ketch agreed to be bought for P. 300.

Agreed that the Diana Ketch be bought at Three [hun]dred Pagodas for the Companys service, and the President payes for the same out of Cash, as alsoe the Charges for the present expedition.

Mr. Raworth added to examine into yᵉ. Town wall assessmᵗ.

Agreed that Mʳ. Raworth be added to Mʳ. Fraser and Mʳ. Meverell in the roome of Mʳ. Marshall to examine into the unequall assessment that was lately made for Building the Black Town Wall and Workes.

100 Ca. salt Petre ordered for Gunpowder.

Ordered that the Warehousekeeper delivers to the Storekeeper One Hundred Candy of Salt Petre to [refine] Gunpowder.

Collaway & Vinkattee Chittees contract for Long Cloth ordd.

how to be paid. reasons for allowing abatements on old Prizes.

Refuse to Contract for a any certain number of peices. [Sallam] pores and Betteelas musters of each produced.

Colloway Chittee and Vinkattee Chittee appeared [this]day as ordered to treat about the price of Long Cloth with whom after a long Debate, 'twas agreed to give them Thirty one Pagodas a corge upon the Muster now before us, Term'd to be Nᵒ. 1. Nᵒ. 2 Pagod[as] Twenty nine and Nᵒ. 3. Twenty seaven Pagodas, the Length of which to be 72 Covᵈˢ., and 2¼ [broad when] Brown ; to be paid in part when brought in and the Account to be cleared as soon as washed and sorted. We were in great hopes to have agreed for the aforesaid Longcloth at Pagᵃ. 30 ⅌ Corge, but they alledged that whereas they were to send their own money into the Country, and run all risgoes from the Government, and not to be paid till the Goods were brought in and sorted, 'tis very much [more] to their disadvantage then the usuall Contracts the Company formerly made, besides they utterly refused to agree for any certain Number of Pieces; supposing their intent thereby is that they would bring in no more then as they saw their advantage thereon : They also produced musters of Sallampores and forty Covᵈˢ. Betteelaes which were not approved of so promised to bring others.

Tʜᴏ. Pɪᴛᴛ.
Wɪʟʟ. Fʀᴀsᴇʀ.
Tʜᴏ. Wʀɪɢʜᴛ.
Jᴏʜɴ Mᴇᴠᴇʀᴇʟʟ.
Tʜᴏˢ. Fʀᴇᴅᴇʀɪᴄᴋ.
Rᴏʙᵀ. Rᴀᴡᴏʀᴛʜ.

4ᵗʰ.

The Governour received last night newes from Pollicherry of the arrivall there of a small ship from France who give out they expect four more of considerable strength two Men of Warr and two Companys ships.

11ᵗʰ.

Ship Johanna Coja Satoor Noquedah sailed out of yᵉ. read for Fort Sᵗ. David and Atcheen.

———————

Aᴛ ᴀ Cᴏɴsᴜʟᴛᴀᴛɪᴏɴ

Present

Tʜᴜʀsᴅᴀʏ, 6ᵗʰ.

Tʜᴏᴍᴀs Pɪᴛᴛ Esqˢ. Pʀᴇsɪᴅᴇɴᴛ & Govˢ.
Wɪʟʟɪᴀᴍ Fʀᴀsᴇʀ.   Tʜᴏᴍᴀs Wʀɪɢʜᴛ.
Jᴏʜɴ Mᴇᴠᴇʀᴇʟʟ.   Tʜᴏᴍᴀs Fʀᴇᴅᴇʀɪᴄᴋ.
Rᴏʙᴇʀᴛ Rᴀᴡᴏʀᴛʜ.

Pa. 1000 pd. into cash Account Sea. Customs.

Mʳ. Thomas Wright payes into the Rᵗ. Honᵇˡᵉ. Companys Cash One Thousand Pagodas in par[t] of the Ballance of Mʳ. Thomas Marshall's Sea Custom account.

——FORT ST. GEORGE, JULY 1704——

and farther payes One Hundred seaventy six Pagodas twenty fanams for fourteen months Town Conico[ply's] duty at the Sea Gate ending ultimo December [last]

P. 176. 20.
pd. into Cash
Accot. Town
Conicoply
duty.

Generall Letter to M^r. William Tillard at Metchlepatam dated yesterday now read and approved.

Letter sent
read.

The Governour acquaints the Council that the Phousdar of S^t. Thoma had released Coja Timore Armenian who he had so unjustly detained [upon] the complaints of Coja Awan.

[Phousdr.]
S^t. Thoma
released Coja
Timore.

Agreed that the Governour has the sole direction of the Diana Ketch as to her fitting, and send her where he thinks most proper for the Companys Interest, with such directions and Instructions as he shall think necessary, and if he sees convenient any one of the Comp^{as}. Factors or writers upon Her.

Diana Ketch
to be soly
under the
direction of
the Govr.

Agreed that an old Grey Horse sent from Metchlepatam formerly belonging to the New Company be sold to M^r. Matthew Mead for one Hundred Pags.

Grey Horse
agreed to be
sold.

> THO. PITT.
> WILL. FRASER.
> THO. WRIGHT.
> JOHN MEVERELL.
> THO^s. FREDERICK.
> ROB^T. RAWORTH.

Sloop Diana Capt. Ridgley Comand^r. sailed out of this road.

This day ship Scipio Capt. Burrish Comand^r. arrived in this road from England bound to the Bay but touchd here for water and refreshment, many of his men being down, He advises that there was two ships come out bound for this Port The Martha and Neptune the former he left off of Lisbon and the latter came out ten dayes before him in Company with the Fleet y^t. carryed the King of Spain to Portugall.

11th.
12.

S^t. Georges Ketch Capt. William Weld Comand^r. arrived in this road from York Fort, by whom received a Generall Letter from the Governour and Council there dated 29th May last.

14.

Briggantine Endeavour Capt. Hart Com^r. arrived in y^s. road from Battavia.

To [CAPTAIN] BURRISH COMAND^R.

OF SHIP [SCI]PIO IN MADRASS ROAD.

We have sent off Messrs. Meverell and Raworth two of our Council with our Secretary desiring you will permitt them in your presence to open the Company's Packet for Bengall not only that for the United[Trade] but also that for the Separate Affaires of the Old Company and take out what Packets directed for this Place, which may be of great moment to the Companys affaires, and afterwards to be made up and sealed as before. There will also come on board you three Armenians with a Chest of Silver containing 21,000 Rupees which wee desire you to take on board you for Account of the U[nited] Trade, and give them Bills of Loading for the same having adjusted the freight one ⅌ Cent to be paid [to] their Council in Bengall Dated in Fort S^t. George 15th July 1704.

> THOMAS PITT.
> WILLIAM FRASER.
> THOMAS WRIGHT.
> JOHN MEVERELL.
> THOMAS FREDERICK.
> ROBERT RAWORTH.

Ship Dansburgh arrived in this road from Trincombar.

15

——————

h

—FORT ST. GEORGE, JULY 1704—

AT A CONSULTATION

Present

<table>
<tr><td rowspan="3">TUESDAY
18th.</td><td colspan="2">THOMAS PITT ESQ^R. PRESIDENT & GOVERNOUR.</td></tr>
</table>

TUESDAY
18th.

THOMAS PITT ESQ^R. PRESIDENT & GOVERNOUR.
WILLIAM FRASER. , THOMAS WRIGHT.
JOHN MEVERELL. THOMAS FREDERICK.
ROBERT RAWORTH.

[Account] Cash for June read.	Thomas Pitt Esqr. President reads his Account of the R^t. Honble. United Companys Cash for the month of June last Ballance Pagod^s. 43613 : 12 : 5.
[Ps. 400] p^d. into Cash for rent [of the New] Townes.	Seraupau payes into the R^t. Honble. United Comp^s. Cash the sum of Four Hundred Pagodas in part of the Rent for the New Townes.
[Wareho]use Acc^{ot}. for April & May read.	M^r. Thomas Wright Warehousekeeper reads his Warehouse Account for the months of April and May last.
Storekeepers Acc^{ot}. for April & May read.	M^r. Robert Raworth Storekeeper reads his storekeepers Account for the months of April and May last.
Land Custom Acc^{ot}. for June read &	M^r. Thomas Frederick Land Customer reads his Land Custom Account for the month of June last Viz^t.

Choultry Custom	...	...	...	...	Pag^s.	447 : 25 : 55.
Rubie Broakers	...	...	...	...	,,	11 : 24 : 60
Town Broakers	...	...	...	...	,,	9 : 23 : 1
Registring Slaves	...	...	...	...	,,	2 : 8
						471 : 9 : 36

[Ps. 710] paid in on y^t. Account.	and payes into the R^t. Honble. United Companys [cash the sume of] [seven] hundred and Ten Pagod^s. on that account.
P. 250 p^d. into Cash for two horses sold.	M^r. Addison payes into the R^t. Honble. United Company's Cash the sume of One Hundred and fifty Pagodas for a Horse sold him by order of Council, and M^r. Lister pays Two hundred Pagod^s. for a Horse sold him. M^r. Mea[d] payes into Cash One Hundred Pagod^s. for a Horse sold him.
West Coast L^{re} read, and Bills considered of.	Generall Letter from the Governour and Council of Bencoolen dated 29th May last was now read, adviseing of their having drawn Bills upon us to the Amount of Doll^s. 4379 : 2, which Bills were now presented for acceptance, the consideration of which is referred to our [next] Consultation.
P. 44. 24 p^d. into Cash for Salt Pork sold.	M^r. William Jennings Steward payes into the Right Honble. United Companys Cash Fourty four Pagod^s 24 fa. for salt pork sold to the shipping.
Pa. 1000 ordered the Paym^r.	Agreed that One Thousand Pagod^s. be paid to M^r. John Meverell Paymaster to defray Charges Garrison.
[Coja] Timore Petitions for the money attacht in Court belonging to Usuph be p^d. him. deferr'd to next Friday.	Coja Timore delivers in this day his Petition de[sireing] that the money and Goods attach'd by the Court of Admiralty for Account of Coja Usuph whose Attorney, he is, may be delivered him, the examination of which business is deferred to Fryday next at 8 in the morning when all the Armenians are to attend, and M^r. Mead to give them notice of the same.

——FORT ST. GEORGE, JULY 1704 ——

The Governour acquaints the Council that the Chief Minister in Mangamaus Country had made satisfaction for what was seized of Narrains &c⁰. Inhabitants of this Place, for which some Goods belonging to the subjects of that Country were seized as reprizall here which the Governour cleared as soon as Narraia advised him he had received satisfaction. Governʳ. acquaints that the Goods seizd belonging to Mangamans Country are released & why

> THO. PITT.
> WILL: FRASER.
> THO: WRIGHT.
> JOHN MEVERELL.
> THOˢ. FREDERICK.
> ROBᵀ. RAWORTH.

Ship Mary Capᵗ. Samuel Heaton Comandʳ. arrived in this road from Battavia. 19

Ship Riseing Sun Capᵗ. Wyburgh arrived in this road from Holland belong- 20 ing to the Seperate Stock.

Ship Humphrey and Charles Capᵗ. Wright Comandʳ. sailed out of this road 21 for Vizagapatam by whom sent Two Packets to the Cheif and Council there, for the United and Seperate Affaires.

Ketch Tibby Capᵗ. Weoley Com̃ʳ. sailed for the Coast of Syndee.

AT A CONSULTATION

Present

THOMAS PITT ESQ̄ᴿ. PRESIDENT AND GOVERNOUR.
WILLIAM FRASER.   THOMAS WRIGHT.
JOHN MEVERELL.   THOMAS FREDERICK.
ROBERT RAWORTH.

FRIDAY 22.

Thomas Pitt Esqʳ. as Mintmaster reads his Mint Account for the month of June and payes into the Rᵗ. Honᵇˡᵉ. United Companys Cash Fifty four Pagˢ. thirty two fanams forty Cash on that Account. [Mint] Account read and [54]: 32: 40 pd. in on yᵗ Accoᵗ.

Mʳ. Thomas Wright payes into the Rᵗ. Honᵇˡᵉ. United Companys Cash the sume of One Thousand Pagodˢ. in part of the Ballance of Mʳ. Thomas Marshalls Sea Custom Account. Pa. 1000 pdˢ into Cash Account Sea Customs.

Ordered that Antonio de Rosera Topaz be Entertain'd Souldier in this Garrison. A Souldier Entertaind.

Seraupaus Lease for Three Years for the the New Towns being expired from the first of this month, the head inhabitants of which were now before us, and acquainted that the Townes were in the Companys hands, and that [speedily] we would order a supervisoʳ thereof, and that Seraupau had no more to do with them. Seraupaus Lease for the New Towns ended & Inhabitants acquainted therewith.

This day we tooke into our consideration whether we should pay the Bills drawn on us by the Governour & Council of Bencoolen Amounting to Dollˢ., 4379 : [2 : thô] they are drawn on us in the same manner as those [that came] by ship Queen without distinguishing by their [Letter] [or] Bill whether they are for Account of the Old Company or the United Trade, but we considering that these Payment of the West Coast Bills debated.

h-1

Agreed to be paid.   Bills can be for no other Account then the United Trade, and [by rea] son of the small Amount thereof, and that if we [return] them Protested there will be an Interest due upon them, all which induced us to come to this resolution of paying them; And 'tis unanimously agreed they are forthwith paid.

THO : PITT.
WILL : FRASER.
THO : WRIGHT.
JOHN MEVERELL.
THOˢ. FREDERICK.
ROBᴿ. RAWORTH.

Received ꝑ Pattamars the following Generall Letters Vizᵗ.
From the Governᵣ. and Council at Trincombᵣ. datᵈ. 24ᵗʰ July S. N.
From the Governᵣ. and Council at Negapatᵐ. datᵈ. 26   Dᵒ. S. N.
From Depᵗʸ. Governoᵣ. &c. at Fort Sᵗ. David datᵈ. 19ᵗʰ Instant.

AT A CONSULTATION

MONDAY
24ᵀᴴ.

Present

THOMAS PITT ESQᵣ. PRESIDENT & GOVERNᵣ.
WILLIAM FRASER.   THOMAS WRIGHT.
JOHN MEVERELL.   THOMAS FREDERICK.
ROBERT RAWORTH.

[Letrs.] recd. read.   The following Generall Letters were now read Vizᵗ.
From the Governᵣ. and Council of Negapatᵐ. 26 July S. N.
From the Governour & Council of Trincombᵣ. 24 July S. N.
From the Depᵗʸ. Goverᵣ. &cᵃ. at Fort Sᵗ. David datᵈ. 19ᵗʰ Instant.

[Ps. 6000] ordered for Fort Sᵗ. David.   Agreed that six Thousand Pagodˢ. be sent by Peons overland to Fort Sᵗ. David.

[Ps. 56½ pd. into Cash for 3 old [hor]ses sold.   Mᵣ. John Meverell Paymaster payes into the Rᵗ. Honᵇˡᵉ United Companys Cash the sume of Fifty. six Pagˢ. and a Half for three old mangey Horses received from Metchlepatam from the New Companys Factory, and sold here by Publick Outcry.

Wyburgh produces Certificate for Trade.   Capᵗ. Thomas Wyburgh Com̃andᵣ. of ship Riseing Sun produces his Certificate from the Company for liberty to Trade in the East Indies.

Pa 600 pd. into Cash by the Arrac Farmers.   Peter de Pomera &cᵃ. Arrac Farmers payes into the Rᵗ. Honᵇˡᵉ. United Companys Cash the sume of Six hundred Pagodas on that Account.

Petition of Coja Timore heard.   This Day we heard the Petition of Coja Timores, and examin'd matters relating to him and Coja Awan, and upon a full examination of all Papers, and Persons upon oath we came to the following resolutions.

Coja Timores case stated.   First. That Coja Usuphs Letter of Attorney to Coja [Timore] is very Authentick wherein he gives full power to Coja Timore to receive his Effects from Coja Awan which were left in his hands by Coja Paulo.

Secondly. It appears to us that Coja Timore who [came] over with the aforesaid Power in August last on ship Colchester, that soon after he showing the same to Coja Awan, who upon sight thereof promised a due com[plyance] therewith and few dayes after he paid Coja Timore a considerable sumo of money on that Account, who from time to time dunn'd him for the adjustment of all

------FORT ST. GEORGE, JULY 1704------

Coja [Usuphs] Accounts, and that he would deliver him all Papers and obligations relating thereto, which he delayed till [the 20th.] of January, upon which Coja Timore tooke a [Warrant] out of the Court of Admiralty to Arrest Coja Awan who then promised him to deliver him Coja Usuph's [effects] and all Papers relating thereto, and the 25th of [the said month] complyed therewith in delivering up severall [papers] and a full Account of the particulars of Coja [Usuphs] effects signed and sealed by himself, and two [Wittnesses] thereto; Declaring therein that all those effects [were for] Account of Coja Usuph, and that he had nothing [to] demand out of them, but the Commissions of the severall Adventures when they should arrive. When about 40 dayes after the delivery up of the aforesaid Papers, Coja Timore as mentioned in former Consultations went to St Thoma, where he was presently followed by Coja Awan who had an understanding with the Governour of that Place, who clapt up Coja Timore, and used him barborously, demanding of him the Papers which Coja Awan delivered him, which as soon as heard of here were secured in the Court of Admiralty, also the money that arrived on an Armenian ship from Manilha amounted to Pags. 10074 part of wch. amounting to Pags. 3228 : 18. has been paid away by ye. Court of Admiralty as ⅌ the Register appears, so that there remaines Pagods. 6845 : 18 : now in the Companys Cash, with the Papers delivered in at the same time, wch. is unanimously agreed to be paid and delivered to Coja Timore, it appearing plainly to us to be part of the Estate of Coja Usuph whose attorney Coja Timore is. 'Tis farther agreed that the House which appears to us to be Coja Usuphs, in which Coja Awan lived, that Mr. Mead and the Register of the Court of Admiralty gives Coja Timore possession and likewise deliver him the Bale Goods belonging to Coja Usuph as mentioned in Coja Awans List of Goods delivered to Coja Timore, and whereas it appears by Coja Awans List to Coja Timore that there is likewise in the house three & a half Bales belonging to Coja Phanuse [Armenian]. 'Tis ordered that those be also delivered the Person [being] before us this day to demand them, and whatever [Bales] or other Goods that are in the House properly belonging to Coja Awan, 'Tis ordered that Mr. Mead and Mr. [Warr] go and take an Account thereof and seal and lock up the same in a roome apart in that House, and [return] to the President and Council an Account thereof.

THO. PITT.
WILL . FRASER.
THO : WRIGHT.
JOHN MEVERELL.
THOs. FREDERICK.
ROBr. RAWORTH.

Received ⅌ pattamars via Metchlepatam a Generall Letter from Sr. Nicholas Wait &ca. Council at [Surat] dated 31st. May advising the arrivall of the Two men [of warr] at Bombay as also the Josiah. The two [former haveing] lost their Commanders and severall of the[ir men].

Recd. ⅌ Pattamars a Generall Letter from [Mr. Tillard] dated [*Lacuna*] Instant.

AT A CONSULTATION

Present

[TUES]DAY 25th.

THOMAS PITT ESQr. PRESIDENT & GOVERNr.
WILLIAM FRASER.   THOMAS WRIGHT.
JOHN MEVERELL.   THOMAS FREDERICK.
ROBERT RAWORTH.

Agreed that Twelve Hundred Pagodas be paid to the Governour of St. Thoma with the usuall Present, it being the Annuall Rent for this Town, The Kings Duan having wrote the President for the same, who will see that the accustomary receipts be given.

[Ps. 1200] to be paid [Town] rent money.

-----*FORT ST. GEORGE, JULY 1704*-----

[Genll.
Ltres.]
received
read.

Generall Letter from S^r. Nicholas Wait &c^a. Council at Surat dated 31st. May last now read, as also a Gen^{ll}. from M^r. Tillard at Metchlepatam dated [*lacuna*] Instant now read.

THOMAS PITT.
WILL : FRASER.
THO : WRIGHT.
JOHN MEVERELL.
THO^s. FREDERICK.
ROB^t. RAWORTH.

Dispatchd ♏ Pattamars a Generall Letter to the Deputy Governour and Council of Fort S^t. David dated Yesterday.

27TH

About eight this morning we descryed a saile to the Southward, who came to an Anchor beyond S^t. Thoma at 5 in the evening when the President received a Note from Her acquainting him that it [was] ship Martha Capt. Samuel Goodman Comander [who came] directly from England bound to this Port, and [in her] Passage had mett with the misfortune of [loosing her] Mainmast 400 Leagues to the Westward of the [Cape] that she had lost near forty men, souldiers, [sailors] and Laskars, and the surviving but in a miserable condition, having not above Ten well men to work the ship upon which the President immediately ordered Lascarrs to be got ready to send on board Her.

AT A CONSULTATION

Present

FRIDAY
28TH

THOMAS PITT ESQ^r. PRESIDENT & GOV^r.
WILLIAM FRASER.   THOMAS WRIGHT.
JOHN MEVERELL.   THOMAS FREDERICK.
ROBERT RAWORTH.

About Ten this morning arrived the Pa[cquet from] Ship Martha [upon] which the Council was [duly] summon'd when the Packet was open'd wherein was found all Papers as ♏ List Enter'd after this Consultation, and the Generall Letter was now read and all other Papers perused.

Agreed that One Thousand Pagod^s. be paid M^r. John Meverell Paymaster to defray Charges Garrison.

THO. PITT.
WILL : FRASER.
THO : WRIGHT.
JOHN MEVERELL.
THO^s. FREDERICK.
ROB^t. RAWORTH.

LIST OF THE PACKET TO Y^e. FORT ♏ MARTHA.

N^o: 1. Companys Generall to the Fort dat^d. 26th. January 1703.
2. Copy of Comp^s. Gen^{ll}. to D^o. dated 6th. Jan^{ry}. 1703 ♏ Neptune.
3. Invoice of the Martha Amounting to £ 73767 : 13 : 11.
4. Bill of Loading of Ditto.
5. Charterparty of said ship.
6. List of Goods to be provided on the Coast.
7. Copy of the Supra Cargoes Covenants of the Loyall Cooke.
8. Manifest of Goods Lycenced to be ship'd on y^e. Martha.
9.   Ditto on the Loyall Cooke.
10. Manifest of Entries on board y^e. Separate Stock ships.

——*FORT ST. GEORGE, JULY 1704*——

11. Invoices of Medicines to be sent in a Pack^t. [apart.]
12. Companyes Indulgence.
13. Keys of Medicines in the Box apart 3 N°. A for Fort [S^t. George] and 3 N°. C for Fort S^t. David.
14. Covenants of M^r. Anthony Etterick to be a Factor dated the 23^d. December 1703, with his security Bond & Bond to perform Covenants, which being Executed are to be returned us.
15. Copy Orders of Investments for Loy^{ll}. Cooke for Amoy and the Fort.
16. Packet Directed to the President and Council for [affairs] of the Governour and Company of Merch^{ts}. &c^a. at Fort S^t. George.
17. Packet to the Bay to be forwarded thither with the [ship as] also the Charterparty for their guidance.

At a Consultation

Present

SATURDAY 29th

THOMAS PITT ESQ^R. PRESIDENT & GOVERNOUR.
WILLIAM FRASER.   THOMAS WRIGHT.
JOHN MEVERELL.   THOMAS FREDERICK.
ROBERT RAWORTH.

Generall Letter from Commodore Brabourne &c^a. Councill at Anjengo dated the primo Instant, advising the unfortunate newes of ship Neptune Capt. Lesly Comander being lost at Mannacurra on Cape Commareen the 21st. June last in the night, within twenty or [thirty] yards of the shore, the People all saved but one who were arrived at Anjengo, and that M^r. Cowes [one of] their Council was sent down to the wreck to [endea]vour to recover what came ashore from the natives which Letter was now read, as also a Letter from the Command^r. to the Governour and Council here.

Gen^{ll} Lettr. from Anjengo advising the unfortunate loss of Ship Neptune read.

THO: PITT.
WILL: FRASER.
THO: WRIGHT.
JOHN MEVERELL.
THO^s. FREDERICK.
ROB^T. RAWORTH.

At a Consultation

Present

[AUGUST]
[TUESDAY]
p^{mo}.

THOMAS PITT ESQ^R. PRESIDENT & GOVERN^R.
WILLIAM FRASER.   THOMAS WRIGHT.
JOHN MEVERELL.   THOMAS FREDERICK.
ROBERT RAWORTH.

Ordered that the Warehousekeeper do inquire w^t. price Pegue stick Lack is at, and what quantity in Town, and report the same, The Company having ordered some to be bought.

[Price stick] lack to be inquired.

Ordered that the Warehousekeeper loads on board ship Martha her Charterparty of Redwood.

Redwood on board [Martha]

Ordered that M^r. Meverell enquires what [Prisoners] are on the Choultry, and the reason of their being [there, and] report the same to this board.

What Prisoners on the Choultry enquired into.

Paymasters
Account
read.

M^r. John Meverell Paymaster read his Pay[master's] Account for the month
of June last Viz^t.

Charges Garrison	...	...	...	Pag^s. 1229 : 27 :	[. . .]
Charges Cattle	...	...	...	86 : 16 :	[. . .]
Silk Wormes	...	...	...	5 : 5 :	[. . .]
Charges Extraordinary...	...	...		1 : 28 :	[. . .]
Charges Dyett and allowances		...		281 : 10 :	[. . .]
Stores	...	...	...	139 : 33 :	[. . .]
Charges Generall	...	...	...	354 : 31 :	[. . .]
West Coast	...	...	...	150 : 13 :	[. . .]
Ketch Huglyana	...	...	...	262 : 23 :	[. . .]
Factors Provisions	...	...	...	6 : 13 :	[. . .]
Fortifications and repairs	...	...		98 : 12 :	[. . .]

Pag^s. 2616 : 31 : [.   .   .]

Tobacco
farmers pay
in Pa. 583 :
12 on that
Account

Ponagettee Narso &c^a. Tobacco and Beetle farmers [pays] into the R^t. Honble.
United Companys Cash the sume of [Five]hundred eighty three Pagod^s. twelve
fanams on y^t. account.

Persons
employ'd
about ye. silk
wormes
order'd to be
discharged &
the Houses
and Gardens
to be sold.

'Tis ordered that the Paymaster discharge all the [Persons] that are employed
about the silk Wormes for the reasons [enter'd] in our Consultation p^{mo}. May, and
that the Houses [that] were built, and Garden that was fenced in $_{for}$ that purpose
be put up at Outcry, the Paymaster first delivereing into the President and Council the charge of the Houses and Garden.

[Prizes Bet]
teelaes and
Sallampores]
agreed on.

Colloway Chittee and Vinkattee Chittee produced to us y^s. day musters of
Betteelaes and Sallampores, upon which we came to the following Agreement with
them.

Co.
Betteelaes 40.   Long 2⅛ Broad N°. 26 att Pag^s, 32 ⅌ Corge.
Ditto   N°. 25 att Pag^s. 30 ⅌ Corge.

Co.
Betteelaes 50.   Long 2⅛ Broad N°. 29 att Pag^s. 40 ⅌ Corge.
Ditto   N°. 28 att Pag^s. 37 ⅌ Corge.

Co.
Sallampores ord^{ry}. 32 Lo. 2¼ Br^d. N°. 1 att Pag^s. 15 ⅌ Corge.

[Difficulties]
interferring,
incourage-
ments to be
given.

It has not been with a little difficulty that we have perswaded the foregoing
Persons to undertake the Companys Investment, by reason of our not advancing
money as formerly, so to incourage them to bring in Goods in the manner the
Honble. Mannagers have directed without Impressing money. 'Tis agreed for
their incouragement that as soon as they bring in any Long Cloth Brown into the
Godown they are to be paid one Pag^o. ⅌ piece, Half a Pag^o. a piece on Sallampores, and one Pagoda a piece on Betteelaes, and so in proportion of any other
sort of Cloth, which is to be signified in writing by the Warehousekeeper to the
President, who is to pay the same, and as soon as wash'd and sorted the Account
to be cleared.

T$_{HO}$: P$_{ITT}$.
W$_{ILL}$: F$_{RASER}$.
T$_{HO}$: W$_{RIGHT}$.
J$_{OHN}$ M$_{EVERELL}$.
T$_{HOS}$: F$_{REDERICK}$.
R$_{OB}^r$. R$_{AWORTH}$.

———*FORT ST. GEORGE, AUGUST 1704*———

AT A CONSULTATION

Present

THOMAS PITT ESQ^R. PRESIDENT & GOV^R.
WILLIAM FRASER.   THOMAS WRIGHT.
JOHN MEVERELL.   THOMAS FREDERICK.
ROBERT RAWORTH.

WEDNES-
DAY 2.

Sunca Rama and Ramdos &c^a. this day was [before] us, who promised to bring in severall sorts of Cloth fitting for the Companys Investment, so acquainting them on what termes it must be, to which they answered [they] would forthwith provide musters.

Merchants propose the bringing in of Cloth.

This day the Portguez Inhabitants Deli[vered] in a Petition as Entered after this Consultation [the pur]port being concerning the Probiat of Wills, [which wee] lately tooke out of their Padres Hands of [this place] to preserve their Effects falling into the hands of the Patriarch ; The farther consideration of which petition is deferrred to another opportunity.

Portguez Inhabitants deliver in a Petition.

THO: PITT.
WILL: FRASER.
THO: WRIGHT.
JOHN MEVERELL.
THO^s. FREDERICK.
ROB^T. RAWORTH.

To THE HON^{BLE}. THOMAS PITT ESQ^R.
      GOVERN^R. OF FORT S^T. GEORGE &c^a.
      AND TO THE GENTLEMEN OF COUNCIL.

The Humble Petition of those of the Portguez Nation, and other Roman Catholicks Inhabitants of this City of Madrass, to whose notice it came, that your Honour and Council had determin'd that all Wills and Testaments should be approved at the Court of the Honourable Company, which is a thing has not been used for the space of sixty two Yeares, but have alwayes been done before the Capuchine Padres which have been in this Church, as First by the R^d. P^a. Ephram de Nevers (and after his death) by the R^d. P^a. Miguel Anjo, to this very day; with the Consents of all the Governours y^t. have Govern'd this Fort of S^t. George. And seeing that the R^t. Honble. Company has consented that the Inhabitants which Inhabit in their Territorys shall be Judged according to the Customs of the Lawes of each respective Nation, and that the Poverty of your Petitioners is such, that the Charges of their Wills and Testaments being made, or proved in the R^t. Honble. Comp^s. Court should be a great charge to your Petitioners by the delations made in the Court, caused by the multiplicity of Affairs done in it.

Therefore your Humble Petitioners beg of your Hon^r. & Council to have regard to their humble Petition, & Grant them [that their] Wills and Testaments may be done before the [Rev. Padre as was] usuall to this very day, wch. favour [your humble Petitioners hope] to receive from y^r. Hon^r. & Council. Whom God protect in all your affairs.

—FORT ST. GEORGE, AUGUST 1704—

AT A CONSULTATION

Present

SATURDAY
5TH.

THOMAS PITT ESQ^R. PRESIDENT & GOVERNOUR.
WILLIAM FRASER.   THOMAS WRIGHT.
JOHN MEVERELL   THOMAS FREDERICK,
ROBERT RAWORTH.

Vessells to be sent to the Neptunes wreck Men & stores to be provided. · Agreed that the Yatch and Fly we expect from Metchlepatam be sent as soon as convenient after their [arrival] to the Neptunes wreck, with what men, Armes [&] stores they can conveniently carry, and that the President gives orders for the same to be made rea[dy.]

Silver agreed to be sold 16½ Doll ℔ 10 Pags. if coind here and 16¼ if otherways. · Agreed that the Warehousekeeper sell the Comp^ys. silver at sixteen and a half Dollars weight for ten Pagodas to such as coine the same in the Mint, and sixteen and a Quarter Dollars to those who carry it away without Coining it.

Persons agreed to be present at opening the silver. Agreed that the Warehousekeeper Messrs. Meverell and Raworth with the Two Assaymasters be [present] at opening and weighing the silver.

A Souldier and Gunner entertained [20 Gorge] Ordered that Bernard De Mount be Entertained souldier in this Garrison, and Randall Forowke of the Gunroome Cre[w].

[Betteelaes [& ℔d bought] The Governour and Councill haveing view'd the twenty Corge of Bettaelaes offer'd to sale by Colloway Chittee and Vinkattee Chittee, which we find none of the best and very unevenly sorted, and bad wash'd, but to take them together 'Tis Agreed to pay them Twenty seven Pag^s. and a half ℔ corge, they paying for the rewashing of them.

[Betteelaes] at Ps. 42 ℔ corge [agreed] New Muster. Agreed this day with Colloway Chittee and Vinkattee Chittee upon a New Muster of Betteelaes in the Godown N°. A 50 Long and 2¼ Broad at Pagod^s: 42 ℔ Corge Three Hundred pieces to be paid for as brought in.

THO. PITT.
WILL: FRASER.
THO : WRIGHT.
JOHN MEVERELL.
THO^s. FREDERICK.
ROB^T. RAWORTH.

AT A CONSULTATION

Present

[TUE]SDAY
8TH.

THOMAS PITT ESQ^R. PRESIDENT & GOVERN^R.
WILLIAM FRASER.   THOMAS WRIGHT.
JOHN MEVERELL   THOMAS FREDERICK.
ROBERT RAWORTH.

[Warehouse] keeper reports no [Pegue] stick Lack to be [bought] According to an order of Consultation on the primo Instant for the Warehousekeeper to enquire what quantity of Pegue stick Lack is in Town, and the price, who now reports that there is none in this Place.

The following General Letters were now [read and approved].
To Commodore Brabourne &c^a. at Anjengo.
To Capt. John Lesly both dated this day.
To the United Council in Bengall dated yesterday.

————*FORT ST. GEORGE, AUGUST 1704*————

A Letter from the Deputy Govern^r. and Council of S^t. David dated p^{mo}. Instant now read.

There seldome presenting an opportunity for remitting money by Bill from hence to Fort S^t. David, we think it necessary to send them what money possible we can[by] Peons before the Raines. 'Tis therefore Agreed that [six]Thousand Pagod^s. be sent them under the care of [Kisna]dos and twelve Peons, and that timely notice be given to the Deputy Governour at Fort St. David to send some of their Peons to meet ours at Connimeer,[to pre]vent their being any wayes attack'd by the Junkaneers at Boomipollam.

We thinking it the Companys Interest to make some Investment in ordinary Long Cloth and Sallampores at Vizagapatam which will in some measure ease the Charge of that Place. 'Tis therefore Agreed that [Ten Thou]sand Madrass Pagod^s. be sent on a Boat now go[ing] thither under the charge of Ten Peons, and that we write the Chief and Council to draw 5000 Pag^s. more[on us] if they can meet with an opportunity to do the same and that they can Invest it in the aforesaid[goods] but strictly prohibit them not to buy Betteelaes.

Right margin notes:
Pag^s. 6000 agreed to be sent overland to Fort S^t. David by Peons.

Agreed that Pags. 10000 be sent to Vizagapatam to be Investd in Long Cloth ordry. & Sallampores.

Pags. 5000. permitted to be drawn on us, if can inlarge [that] Investment. Betteelaes strictly prohibited.

Kittee Narrain has been often before us about [renting] the Three New Townes Viz^t. Yegmore, Persiawaeke & Tandore, and this day came to an Agreement with him to Lett him a Lease for seven yeares at Thirteen Hundred Pagodas ⅌ Annum, the Company to stand to all Dammages that may accrue from the Government, [by] Armyes or otherwayes, and likewise to allow a considera-tion when it shall happen to be such dry weather when little or no Grain can grow. The Lease for which is Entered after this Consultation, wherein all Terms are more fully expres'd.

Right margin note:
3 new villages to be lat to Narrain for 7 years at Pags. 1300 per annum.

> Tho: Pitt.
> Will : Fraser.
> Tho : Wright.
> John Meverell.
> Thos. Frederick.
> Robt. Raworth.

THIS INDENTURE made this Fifteenth day of August One Thousand seven hundred and four between the President and Council of Fort S^t. George for and in behalf of the R^t. Honble. United English East India Com[p^y.] of the one Part, and Kittee Narrain Gentue Inhabitant of said Place of the other part, WITTNESSETH That the said President and Council as well for and in consideration of the Yearly Rent herein by these presents specified, and reserved as for divers other good [causes and] considerations them the said President and Councill] hereunto especially moveing hath dem[ised granted] and to Farm Letten and by these presents doth [de]mise Grant and to Farm Lett unto the said Kittee Narrain all the three New Townes commonly [called] Yegmore, Persiawake, and Tandore, belonging unto the aforesaid R_{ight} Honble. United English East India Company with all the Ground, Buildings, Gardens and Priviledges within the said Townes, and all the Hedges, Fences and Inclosures thereof, and all [Ap] purtenances and Commoditys whatsoever in [any]wayes, to have and to hold the said Ground, Buildings, Gardens, Priviledges, Hedges, Fences, and commoditys thereof aforesaid with all and singular their appurten-ances to the said Kittee Narrain his Executors Administrators and Assigns from the First of [July] one Thousand seven hundred and four un_{to} the full end and

Right margin note:
[Locus sigilli.]

i-1

———*FORT ST. GEORGE, AUGUST 1704*———

Term of seven yeares without any [im]peachment of any manner of wast, yielding [and] paying therefore yearly and every Year Thir[teen] Hundred Pagodas at one Payment Viz'. on[the primo] July of every year unto the President and Council and the said Kittee Narrain for himself, his Executors Administrators and Assigns, and every of them doth covenant and promise at his and their own [proper] cost and Charges from time to time shall and [will] well and sufficiently repair, ffence, scour, and amend, all the Ground, Buildings, Hedges, Fences & inclosures of the said Townes as often, and when need shall require during the said Term, and the same so well and sufficiently Improved, repaird, ffenced, scour'd and amended in the end of the said Term, shall leave and yield up unto the said President and Council.   And it is hereby farther agreed by and between the said President and Council aforesaid and Kittee Narrain notwithstanding what beforementioned, That if any troubles should happen from the Government of the Country, that then the said President & Council will allow for what he shall make appear to have lost by said troubles, and it is farther agreed that in case of a great drouth, and that the seasonable raines do not fall, that then the President and Council shall [abate] out of the yearly Rent the aforesaid Kittee Narrain what he shall suffer thereby he proveing the same upon oath. And the said Kittee Narrain does hereby farther promise, and Agree that he will sell the aforesaid Company such quantitys of straw from the said Townes as they shall want, paying for the same at Markett price, And the said President and Council doth, covenant, promise and Grant unto the said Kittee Narrain his Heirs Executors Administrators and Assigns upon Payment of the Rent as aforesaid, peaceably and quietly to have hold, occupy and enjoy the said Townes, [Buildings] with all the appurtenances thereunto [belonging during] the said Term of seven years. IN [WITNESS WHERE]of we the President and Council for Account and in behalf of the R'. Honble. United English East [India Company] do hereby oblige ourselves on the one part, and Kittee Narrain for himself on the other part, having hereunto interchangeably sett our Hands and Seals at [Fort S'.] George in the City of Madras the day and year [above] written.

THOMAS PITT.
WILLIAM FRASER.
THOMAS WRIGHT.
JOHN MEVERELL.
THOMAS FREDERICK.
ROB^T. RAWORTH.

AT A CONSULTATION

Present

THOMAS PITT ESQ^R. PRESIDENT & GOV^R.
WILLIAM FRASER.   THOMAS WRIGHT.
JOHN MEVERELL.   THOMAS FREDERICK.
ROBERT RAWORTH.

THURSDAY 10TH.

2000 p^d. in Account Sea custom.

M^r. Thomas Wright payes into the R'. Honble. United Company's Cash the sum of Two thousand [Pagodas] in part of the Ballance of M^r. Thom^s. Marshall's Sea Custom Account.

M^r. Thomas Wright Warehousekeeper acquaints now the President and Council that he has received Two Bales more then Invoiced on board ship Martha markt the United Company [with] mark N°. 38 q'. Cloth rashes red N°. 117: q' Broad cloth ordinary Green, wch. were ordered on board ship Neptune. .

———*FORT ST. GEORGE, AUGUST 1704*———

Ordered thắt M^r. William Fraser, and the Warehousekeeper in the presence of the Commander and Purser of ship Martha view what Bales damaged on said ship, and state the same. [Persons] Ordered to view the [Bales red. ẙ Martha [Damage] to be stated

We fearing that Goods will not be brought in here in so great plenty as to fill up the Tonnage the Company have ordered; 'Tis therefore agreed that the following Investment be made at Fort S^t. David, and that they be immediately advised thereof. [quantity of] Goods to be [brought] at Fort St. Davd.

30000 Pieces Long Cloth ordinary ...	Thirty thousand [pieces]
7500 Pieces of 40 co^{ds}. Betteelaes ...	Seven Thousand five Hundred [pieces]
7500 Piece's of 50 Betteelaes ...	Seven Thousand five hund[red pieces]
15000 Pieces of Sallampores ord^{ry}. ...	Fifteen thousand [pieces]
3000 Pieces Neckcloths ...	Three thousand [pieces]
2000 Pieces Long Cloth Fine if to be had at 50. or 55 Pag^s. a corge and to be sorted by the old Musters.	Two thousand [pieces]
2000 Pieces Fine Sallampores if to be had pro rato	Two thousand [pieces]

Agreed that one Thousand Pagodas be advanced M^r. John Meverell Paymaster for defraying Charges Garrison. [Pa. 1000] advanced y^e. paymaster.

This day Colloway Chittee and [Vincattee Chittee being] before us we acquainted them wi[th the following] [par]ticulars of what Goods we expecte[d them to provide Viz^t.] The quantity Goods Agreed with Colloway Chittee &c^a. who

20000 Pieces Long Cloth ordinary ...	Twenty thousand
10000 Pieces 40 and 50 Cov^d. Betteelaes	Ten thousand pieces.
10000 Pieces of Sallampores ...	Ten thousand pieces
2000 Pieces Long Cloth Fine ...	Two thousand pieces
2000 Pieces Sallampores Fine ...	Two thousand pieces
4000 Pieces all sorts of Moorees ...	Four thousand pieces
2500 Pieces Neck cloths ...	Two thousand five hundred
300 Pieces Betteelaes new muster ...	Three hundred pieces

The Prizes of some of which are before agreed, and they were this day ordered to hasten to bring in Musters of Long cloth fine, Sallampores Fine, Moorees of severall sorts, and after a Long debate with the two aforesaid Persons they told us that unless we prohibited all other [Merchants] in this Town from making Investments in [the like] sorts of Goods, we must not expect they could comply with the same, which they urged so strenuous[ly] and seemed resolved that unless we Granted their [request] they would desist from going any farther in prov[iding] the aforesaid Goods, so to prevent so great a [prejudice] to the Company as disappointing them of their [tonnage] we promise to comply therewith; yet nevertheless shall underhand persist in incourageing all People [to bring] in such Goods as are fit for their Investment. [per] sist to have oth^er Merchts. [forbid] buying up such Goods [and] wh^y agree^d

The Honble. Mannagers having ordered by [the Martha] the buying some Metchlepatam Goods, which [have been] till of late extravagantly dear, but as we are [informed] are now tollerably cheap to what they were, [by reason] of the New Company desisting from making Investments, and [the] Old Companys Factory withdrawn, & fearing that if we should now in pursuance to the Mannagers orders send down Persons as if we intend to settle a Factory for the United Trade which would undoubtedly run up again the prizes of Goods. Tis therefore resolved that we send down Kittee Narrain with Ten thousand Pagodas to buy up such Goods as he shall be directed in our Instructions to him; And that the President payes him out of Ca$h One Hundred and fifty Pagodas towards defraying his charges, and the following things to be sent by him Viz^t. Gold Chains to the value of about 70 Pag^s. Broad Cloth-2 Bales. Narrain goes to Metchlepatm. to Invest [10000 ps.] in chay goods. [Reason for] not settling a [factory at] Metchm. [Pa. 150 paid] towards [charges and Presents to be sent with] him

---

FORT ST. GEORGE, AUGUST 1704———

Aurora 2 p⁵. perpetuanoes red 1 Bale.
Scarlet 10 yards. : Rosewater 1 Chest.
Cloth rashes 1 Bale red. 6 Cases strong Water.
2 Fowling pieces 12 Ivory handled knives.
1 Bale Wax Cloth 1 Bale Dungaree.

[Mr. Faucett] agreed to be [sent to] Metchlepatam; & [Pa. 14 per] mensem to be pᵈ. rim.

There being a necessity of sending a person to Metchlepatam to take care of the Dead Stock for the United Trade we have this day made choice of Mʳ. Thomas Faucett with whom we now agree to pay him monthly in lieu of salary, Dyett, Fourteen pagod⁸ ℔ month and the Company to be at no other charge then the peons they have at the Factorys of Metchlepatam & Maddapollam, to which place of [Matchlepatampa] is to [repaire] by first boat.

Ordered that Mʳ. Hall be Entertaind Doctʳˢ. second Mate.

2 Souldiers & a Gunner Entertaind

Ordered that Antonióde Rosaro be Entertaind one of the Gunners Crew, and Paul de Silvia, and [Anthony Secare] Topazes, be Entertain'd Souldiers in this Gar[rison].

Tho: Pitt.
Will: Fraser.
Tho: Wright.
John Meverell.
Thoˢ. Frederick.
Robᵗ. Raworth.

10
11

Ship Latchee Prasaude Mahomud Hussan Noquedah sailed for Bengall.

Dispatch'd ℔ Peons a Generall Letter to the Governour and Council of Fort Sᵗ. David dated [this] day with 6,000 Pagod⁸. under the charge of [said Peons]

Ship Mary Capᵗ. Cornwall Comandʳ. sailed out of [this] road for Bengall by whom sent a Packet [to the Coun]cil for the United Trade in Bengall dated [the] 8ᵗʰ. Instant:

Ship Rising Sun Capᵗ. Wyburgh Comander sail'd out [of this road for] Bengall.

Received ℔ Pattamars a Generall Letter from Commodore Brabourne &cᵃ. Council at Anjengo datᵈ. 17ᵗʰ. July last.

AT A CONSULTATION

Present

[Tues]day 15ᵗʰ.

Thomas Pitt Esqʳ. President & Governᵣ.
William Fraser. Thomas Wright.
John Meverell. Thomas Frederick.
Robert Raworth.

[Mint Masters acct. for July read.

Thomas Pitt Esqʳ. as Mintmaster reads his Mint Accoᵗ. for the month of July last, and payes into the Rᵗ. Honᵇˡᵉ. United Companys Cash the sum of Ninety five Pagod⁸. Nineteen fanams for Custom on Gold coined.

[Sea Custom account for June read.

Mʳ. Thomas Wright Sea Customer reads for Mʳ. Thomas Marshall the Sea Custom Account for the month of June last Viz⁵.

Custom on Goods Imported and exported this month.					Pa.1,686 :	34 :	72
To Custom on Grain	...	...	...	...	229 :	22 :	4
To Anchorage	...	...	...	...	66 :	18 :	...
To Tonnage	...	...	...	...	194 :	18 :	...

Pag⁸. 2,177 : 18 : 76

————*FORT ST. GEORGE, AUGUST 1704*————

The following Generalls and Instructions were now read and approved, which Instructions are as Enter'd after this Consultation. [Generals] and Instructions read.

    Instructions to Kittee Narrain for his Journey to Metchlepatam.
    Instructions to M^r. Thomas Faucet to reside at Metchlepatam.
    Generall Letter to M^r. Simon Holcombe Chief &^c. Councill at Vizagapatam all Dated this day.

Agreed that the following Goods be sent to Vizag[patam] :—

    1 Bale of Aurora 6 Bales Broad cloth ordinary red.
    6 Bales of Broadcloth ordinary Green.
    1 Bale Cloth rashes red.   1 Bale Ditto Green.
    1 Bale Perpetuanoes red.   1 Bale Ditto Green.

    6 Chests of Syrash Wine 1 Chest Rosewater and that the Ten Thousand Pagodas ord]ered for be now sent] [Viza]gapatam in Consultation the 8th. Instant. with the above things on the S^t. George [Friggat]. Pag^s. 10,000 to be sent to Vizagp^m. on St. George Frigatt.

Generall Letter to M^r. William Tillard at Metchlepatam dated this day.

THO : PITT.
WILL : FRASER.
THO : WRIGHT.
JOHN MEVERELL.
THO^s. FREDERICK.
ROB^r. RAWORTH.

INSTRUCTIONS TO KITTEE NARRAIN FOR HIS JOURNEY TO METCHLEPATAM.

We depending upon your integrity as well as great experience in those parts, have made choice of you to goe to Metchlepatam, where we intend to make a small Investment, provided Goods can be bought much cheaper then formerly, of which by the informations we have had, we have a great prospect.

We forbear at present to send any English to appear in making the Investment fearing it may run up y^e. Goods to the former prizes, besides we are willing to avoid the extraordinary charges that attend a Factory ; We are in great hopes you'l find good part of the Goods we want ready made, so that there will be no need trusting of money into the Merchants Hands, which our Company have possitively ordered the contrary, and therefore we enjoyn you to observe the same.

The Investment we order you to make is as follows :—

    3,000 Pieces of Romalls   ...   .   Three thousand p^s.
    2,000 Peices of Allejars   ...   .   Two thousand p^s.
    1,000 Peices of Sacerguntees   ...   ...   One Thousand p^s.
    1,000 Peices of Collawapooses   ...   ...   One Thousand p^s.

which Goods must be full Lengths and breadths & the best Chay, which you must take care to be well washt, Packt, and be ready to goe Home in January. We shall here in few dayes dispatch a Boat to Metchlepatam with severall things for sale and Pre[sents] under the care of M^r. Faucett who is to reside [there] to receive the Dead stock from the Old and New [Camp^s.] and looke after the same for Account of the New [Trade] for whose Account you goe to make this Investment unto which he is a stranger, tho' we have ordered [him] to countenance you in all your business, and [own all] the Goods bought by you as the Company's [and give] you accommodation not only for Lodgings but Warehouse roome &c^s. in the Factory.

We have no orders from the Company for buying any white Cloth there, yet nevertheless if the Fine Long [cloth] N°. 1. of which there is Musters in the Companys [factory] can be bought between Fifty and sixty Pagod^s. [per corge we would have you buy one Thousand Pieces, [so like]wise the same quantity of fine Sallampores if [they can] be bought pro rato.

————*FORT ST. GEORGE, AUGUST 1704*————

We order you to send us frequent advices [of your] negotiation and write us fully thereof.

We have now paid you One Hundred and [fifty] Pagod⁹. for your expences of which you must give [an] Account at your returne, when we will reward [You] suitable to your merits. Dated in Fort Sᵗ. [George this] eighteenth day of August 1704.

THOMAS PITT.
WILLIAM FRASER.
THOMAS WRIGHT.
JOHN MEVERELL.
THOMAS FREDERICK.
ROBERT RAWORTH.

To Mʳ. THOMAS FAUCETT.

The great hopes we have of your faithfullness and dilligence, induced us to elect you into the United Companys service to goe and reside at Metchlepatam where you are to live in that which was called the Old Companys Factory, and take under your care the Dead stock that formerly belonged to the Old and New Company at Metchlepatam and Maddapollam, which now appertains to the United Trade, an Inventory of both which we now deliver you. The dead stock of the Old Company is in their Factorys, but that belonging to the New is to be delivered you by Mʳ. Tillard to whom we have wrote to send up severall things by the Yatch and Boats of which we deliver you a Copy, which if not sailed before your arrivall we order you to see the severall things put on board them, and hasten the Vessells hither with all expedition.

Kittee Narrain will be at Metchlepatam to negotiate some particular affaires of his own, whom we order you to countenance as if he was the Compˢ. servant, and if he buys any thing to own it as the Companys Goods, we have likewise permitted him to lye in the Factory, and you may accommodate him with Ware-houseroome if he has occasion [or] what else he shall want.

We send under your care severall sorts of Goods &cˢ. which we order you to carry to the Factory and there deliver them to Narrain as he shall demand them. -

Mʳ. Frewen left six servants to looke after the Metchlepatam and Four Servants to looke after the Maddapollam Factorys, which numbers w[e would] have you reduce believing two or three will be sufficient when you are there.

We have agreed with you for fourteen Pagˢ. [per] month in lieu of Salary, Dyett and all charges [what]soever during your residing there, which is [to be at] the pleasure of the President and Council of this place whose orders you are to obey for your returning hither and if we should add a Writer to you, [you are] to be considered Four Pagˢ. ℔ month for his [Dyet] and no more.

We order you to correspond with us by all opportunityes, and when any newes happens of con[sequence] you are to dispatch Peons to us at the Compˢ. charge.

We order you to send up all the Plate reserving only a Beetle box, Rosewater bottle, and Pigdan, [as] also the Pallankeens, keeping there the New Co[mpany's] Seconds and an ordinary one or two for the use of the Factory.

We would have you make no manner of appearance to avoid charges from the Government tho' upon Sundays or ships coming in we would have you hoist Sᵗ. Georges Flag at the Factory.

We would have you tender Mʳ. Tillard the use of both or either of our Factorys to live in, who is also to have the use of the Warehouses.

——FORT ST. GEORGE, AUGUST 1704——

We strictly enjoyn you to looke after every thing very carefully, and air those things that require it to prevent their being spoilt. Dated in Fort S^t. George this Eighteenth day of August 1704.

> Thomas Pitt.
> William Fraser.
> Thomas Wright.
> John Meverell.
> Thomas Frederick.
> Robert Raworth.

P.S.—Desist from takeing any one of the New Companys Servants till our farther Orders.

This evening we spyed a ship coming in from the Northward with a Dutch **17** Flagg at Topmast head, who came almost into the Road just at six, when she saluted the Garrison with seventeen Guns, which were returned with the like number; this ship the President is advised came from Pollicat on whom is Monheer Slyland going to Negapatam to succeed Governo^r. Comans in that Government.

Dutch Ship sailed early y^e. morning. **18**

Briggantine Endeavour Capt. Samuel Hart Commander sailed out of this **19** road for Bengall.

Dispatchd by M^r. Thomas Faucet by Boat the following Packets Viz^t. **20**

To M^r. Tillard at Metchlepatam dated 15th. Instant and the following Packets to Surat to be forwarded thither.

To the Generall and Council at Surat.

To S^r. Nicholas Wait &c^a. Council both dated the [18th. Instant] with Duplicates of our last Letters to Persia.

Received ꝑ Pattamars two Packets from the Deputy Governour and Council of Fort S^t. David dated [16 Instant].

AT A CONSULTATION

Present

> Thomas Pitt Esqr. President & Governour.
> William Fraser. Thomas Wright.
> John Meverell. Thomas Frederick.
> Robert Raworth.

M^r. Thomas Wright Warehousekeeper payes into the R^t. Honble. United Companys Cash the sume of Fifteen Thousand Pagodas on Account Silver and Goods sold out of the Warehouse.

Pa. 15,000, pd. by the Warehouse-keepr for silver & Goods sold.

Thomas Pitt Esqr. President reads his Account of the R^t. Honble. United Companys Cash for the month of July last Ballance Pag^s. 28595 : 30 : 5.

Accot. Cash for July moth. read.

M^r. Robert Raworth Storekeeper reads his Storekeepers Account for the month of July last.

Storekeeprs. Accot. read.

k

—FORT ST. GEORGE, AUGUST 1704—

Land Customers Accoᵗ. July [month] read.

Mʳ. Thomas Frederick Land Customer reads his Land Custom Account for the month of July last.

Choultrey Custom	...	...	...	...	Pa. 345 : 24 : 35
Rubie breakers	...	...	...	...	24 : 27 : 36
Town Broakers	...	...	...	...	11 : 14 : 10
Registring slaves	...	...	...	...	2 : 16 : ...
					Pa. 384 : 10 : 1

[Paid] by the Secretary his fees, and [his] Accots, for moths. [of June and] July read.

Henry Davenport Secretary reads his Account fees for Passes for the months of June and July last, and payes into the Rᵗ. Honᵇˡᵉ. United Companys Cash the sume of sixteen Pagodas on that Account.

[Paid] by Serraubau [Pa. 650 for] the [rent] of the new Towns.

Serraupau payes into the Rᵗ. Honᵇˡᵉ. United Companys Cash the sume of · six Hundred and fifty Pagodᵃ. on Account Rent of the New Townes.

[650 Pᵃ.] agreed to be advanced to Washers.

Agreed that six hundred and Fifty Pagodas be advanced to Paupiah &cᵃ. Washers towards curing the Rᵗ. Honᵇˡᵉ. United Companys Cloth.

[Letter] to Anjengo.

Generall Letter to Commodore Brabourne &cᵃ. Council at Anjengo dated yesterday now read and approved.

Paymasters] [Accoᵗ. moᵗʰ. July.

Mʳ. John Meverell Paymaster reads his Account for the month of July last.

Charges Garrison	...	...	...	Pag.	1,284 : 20 : —
Charges Cattle	...	...	...		64 : 17 : —
Silk Wormes	...	...	...		5 : 26 : —
Charges Extraordinary	...	...			— : 32 : —
Charges Dyett and allowances	...	...			276 : 16 : 20
Stores	...	...	...	...	79 : 21 : 60
Charges Generall	...	...			354 : 31 : —
Charges Merchandize	...	...	...		— : 18 : —
West Coast	...	...	...	...	1 : 9 : —
Fortification and repairs	...	...			170 : 34 : —
					2239 : 9 : —

Genˡˡ. from Fort Sᵗ. David read.

Generall Letter from the Deputy Governour and Council of Fort Sᵗ. David dated 16ᵗʰ. July now read.

Report of w. damaged cloth recᵈ. per ship Martha.

Mʳ. Fraser and the Warehousekeeper report that they had view'd the Cloth received by ship Martha and find the Dammage to be no more then in Bale Nᵒ. [223] Piece 684, and Bale Nᵒ. 44. pᵃ. 130 halfe a piece of which was delivered to the Comandʳ. at Invoice [price] for which he paid the Warehousekeeper for the same.

Pa. 1000 advanced the Paymaster.

Agreed that One Thousand Pagodas be advanced to Mʳ. John Meverell Paymaster to defray Charges Garrison.

A Souldier Entertained.

Ordered that Pasquall de Costa Topaz be Entertained a Souldier in this Garrison.

Ordered that that the Paymaster muster ship [Martha's] Company and report the same.

Attorney Genˡˡ. order'd to seize Coja Awans Goods for Pa. 60: 3C indebt'd for Custm.

Coja Awan who had lately a great contest here [with] Coja Timore when he withdrew hence to Sᵗ. Thoma [which] time he left Customs unpaid Amounting to [60 Pagodas] thirty Fanams, to pay which 'tis ordered that the Attorney Generall and Register extends some of the Goods that lye in Coja Usuphs House, and sell them at the Sea Gate, and what they shall surmount the [aforesaid] sum that he owes be paid into the Companys Cash.

———*FORT ST. GEORGE, AUGUST 1704*———

Agreed that the Governour gives orders to Serjeant Dixon and Serjeant Hugonin to provide themselves to goe with the men that are designed to goe to the Neptunes Wrack.

Serjeant Dixon & Hugonin to go to ye. Neptune wrack.

Cap'. Francisco De Saa dying lately on a Voyage to Battavia, and having left no Will, 'tis ordered y'. Mess'". Wright and Meverell demand and receive of Cap'. Samuel Heaten what money, Goods, Books & Papers in his hands belonging to the said Francisco de Saa and to call Senh'. Francisco Cordoza to their assistance, and that they state his Account, and pay all his Debts, and what shall remain it being according to the Portuguez Law (those that dye Intestate) to pay a moiety to his Widdow and the other moiety into the Companys Cash, which is to lye till demanded by his relations who have a right thereto, who are said to be in Europe and none in those parts.

Mess". Wright & Meverell ordered to take care Senh". of [Saa's effects] and pay a [moiety to] ye. widdow.

M'. Matthew Empson who was formerly one of this Council, and ordered by the Honble. Mannagers to be Second of Fort S'. David, but he finding it very inconvenient to remove thither by reason of his Family & concerns here, He delivered in a Petition this day to be dismiss'd the Companys service, which was accordingly Granted him, and his Petition Enter'd after this Consultatin.

[Empson] Petitions to lay [down the] Comps service agreed he] has leave.

This day agreed with Colloway Chittee and Venkattee Chittee for Twenty Thousand Neckcloths at Twelve for a Pagoda Long 3 Cov^ds, Broad 1½ Cov^ds. when Brown Muster Agreed upon being sealed with the Companys and their seal.

Neckcloths.

We having already sold, and being about to sell more of the Persian Horses belonging to the Old Comp". 'Tis Agreed that we buy four Atcheen horses in the roome thereof at 30 Pag'. a Horse.

Persian horses agreed to be [bought.]

Agreed that Ten thousand Pagodas more be sent overland by Peons to Fort S'. David, [first adviseing] thereof that they may send Peons to meet ours at Connimeer to conduct the same.

Pag" 10,000 agreed to be sent to Fort S'. David.

> THO: PITT.
> WILL: FRASER.
> THO: WRIGHT.
> JOHN: MEVERELL.
> THO". FREDERICK.
> ROB'. RAWORTH.

TO THE HON^BLE. THOMAS PITT ESQ".
    PRESIDENT & GOVERNOUR OF
    FORT S'. GEORGE &c^A. COUNCIL.

S^RS.

Whereas my Honble. Masters [for the United] Company were pleased to confer me to be Second of Fort S'. David, which most certainly they esteem'[d id as a] mark of their favour by so doing.

But it has happend very inconvenient to me [for] the following reasons, because I have been a housekeeper in this Place for Eleven yeares, which has caused me build for the settlement of my Family which is large, having Wife and Children, so that if I should remove hence, it would be of great prejudice to me, I have also lived here. Eighteen yeares by which means it has made me capable of serving their Honours without doubt better here then any where else.

My request to your Honour and Council is that I may have leave to dismiss myself from their Honours service by which means I may sitt still, till their Honours signifie their pleasure how they will dispose of me. I beg the favour of your Honour &c". in permitting this Paper to be Enterd in the Consultation Booke that my Honourable Masters may have the perusall of it in England I am

FORT S'. GEORGE,
    23^D AUGUST 1704.

> Honble. S'. &c".
> Your most Obedient Humble
>   Servant
>   ·MATT: EMPSON

k-1

———FORT ST. GEORGE, AUGUST 1704———

24TH	Ship Bombarupum Cojee Tanerre Noquedah saild for Bengall. Dispatch'd ℞ Pattamarr a Generall Letter to the Deputy Governour and Council of Fort Sᵗ. David datᵈ. this day.
25	Dispatch'd ℞ Pattamarr the following General Lettʳˢ. To Commodore Brabourne &cᵃ. at Anjengo datᵈ. 22ᵈ· Insᵗ. Copyes of our last Letters to Persia to be forwarded thither by Messʳˢ. Harnett and Scattergood now at Tutecoreen.
26	Received ℞ Pattamars a Generall Letter from the Chief and Council of Vizagapatam dated 4ᵗʰ Instant.
27	Dispatch'd a Generall Letter to the Deputy Governour and Council of Fort Sᵗ. David dated this day [with Ten] Thousand Pagodˢ. under the Charge of Kisnados [and twenty] peons.
28	Sᵗ. George Friggot Capᵗ. William Weld Commandʳ. [saild] out of this Road for Vizagapatam and Bengall to the [former] sent a Packet to the Chief and Council there dated the 15ᵗʰ and 26ᵗʰ Instant. Ship Pearle Capᵗ. Twisden Comͧandʳ. sailed out of this [road] for Mallacca.
29	Sloop Hierusalem arrived in this road from Trincombar.
31	Received ℞ Pattamars this day the following Packets. From the United Council in Bengall dated 7ᵗʰ April [and 19ᵗʰ May] and copyes of theirs dated 9ᵗʰ and 23ᵈ March the originals of which never came to Hand. From Vizagapatam dated 13ᵗʰ Instant. From Mʳ. Tillard dated 21ˢᵗ Ditto.

AT A CONSULTATION

Present

SEPTEMBEᴿ FRIDAY PᴹO.	THOMAS PITT ESQᴿ. PRESIDENT & GOVʳ. WILLIAM FRASER. THOMAS WRIGHT. JOHN MEVERELL. THOMAS FREDERICK. ROBERT RAWORTH.

Several Generall Letters recd. now read.	The following General Letters received last night ℞ Pattamars overland were now read. From the United Council in Bengal One Dated 9ᵗʰ March last ⎱ copyes, the originalls never came to Hand. One dᵃted 23ᵈ Ditto. ⎰ One dated the 7ᵗʰ of April. One dated the 19ᵗʰ May. From the Chief and Council of Vizagapataᵐ datᵈ. 13ᵗʰ August. From Mʳ. William Tillard at Metchlepatᵐ. datᵈ. 13ᵗʰ & 21ˢᵗ August.
Answer to yᵉ. Bengall Genll. to be sent. [Ship Martha's] compᵃ. 86 men.	An answere to the Bengall Generalls were now considered of and resolved to send by ship Martha. Paymaster reports ship Marthas Company to be Eighty six men and Boyes.

THO : PITT.
WILL : FRASER.
THO : WRIGHT.
JOHN MEVERELL.
THOˢ : FREDERICK.
ROBᵀ. RAWORTH.

Ship Martha Capᵗ. Samuel Goodman Comͧandʳ. sailed this morning out of this Road for Bengall by whom sent the Following Packets Vizᵗ.
To the United Council in Bengall datᵈ. 31ˢᵗ of August.
To Ditto dated the primo Instant.

——*FORT ST. GEORGE, SEPTEMBER 1704*——

Ship Mahomuddee Mahomud Hussain Noquedah sailed out of this road 3 for Cuddaloor.

Ship Dorothy Cap*t*. Ford Co*mand*. sailed out of this road for Pegue.

Briggantine Destiny Cap*t*. Edwards Com*r*. sailed for [Pegue].

Ship Charlton Cap*t*. Gostlin Co*mand*. arrived in this road from Bombay, having Lost his passage hither and laid two months at Carwarr, by whom received a Generall Letter from S*r*. John Gayer &c*n*. at [Surat] dated 25th April 1704. Two Generalls from the Deputy Governour and Council of Bombay dated 13th & [16th May] last.

Received this day two Letters from the Deputy [Gov*r*.] and Council of Fort St. David dated 31st August [and 2*d*.] Instant with their Generall Bookes A and B.

AT A CONSULTATION

Present

THOMAS PITT ESQ*R*. PRESIDENT & GOV*R*.
WILLIAM FRASER. THOMAS WRIGHT.
JOHN MEVERELL. THOMAS FREDERICK.
ROBERT RAWORTH.

MONDAY 4TH

Ponagettee Narso &c*a*. Tobacco and Beetle farmers pays into the R*t*. Hon*ble*. United Companys Cash the sume of Five hundred eighty three Pagodas and twelve fanams on that Account.

*Pa. the 583: 12. p*d*. in by the Tobacco Farmers.*

M*r*. Thomas Wright Sea Customer payes into the Rt. Hon*ble*. United Companys Cash the sume of One thousand Pagod*s*. on Accot. Sea Customs.

Pa. 1000 pd. in Sea Custom Account

Serraupau payes into the Rt. Hon*ble*. United Companys Cash the sume of Four Hundred Pagod*s*. on Account Rent of the New Townes.

[Pa. 400 pd.] by Serraupau Rent New Townes.

Agreed that Ten thousand Pagod*s*. more be sent by Peons to Fort St. David, and that advices be sent beforehand for Peons to meet ours at Connimeer to conduct it.

[Pa. 10000] agreed to be sent to Fort St. David.

We having in severall Letters since the arrivall of the Martha press'd the Deputy Governour and Council of Fort S*t*. David to come to a speedy conclusion with their Merchants for the prizes of Goods in the method ordered by the Hon*ble*. Managers and having advised them of the prizes we give here about which they write they have had severall conferences with their Merchants, but cannot bring them to agree on the same Termes; so considering the time is short to provide so considerable a quantity of Goods ['Tis] agreed that we write them that they forthwith conclude on the best termes they can, and advise thercof.

[Fort St.] David to agree with [their] Merchts for an investment [ment] on the best terms they can.

Agreed that Two hundred Pagod*s*. be advanced M*r*. Robert Raworth Storekeeper towards making of Powder.

[Pa. 200] advanced Storekeeper to make Powder

Agreed that One Thousand Pag*s*. be advanced M*r*. John Meverell Paymaster towards defraying Charges Garrison.

[Pa. 1000] advanced the Paymr.

M*r*. Stephen Frewen payes into the Rt. Hon*ble*. United Companys Cash the sume of Two hundred Pag*s*. [for Money pay*d* in by] the Inhabitants towards building [the Black Town] Wall and Works.

[Pa. 200 pd. in] by the Inha [bitants.]

Ordered that Venture Desire, Manuel Caldera and Francisco de Costa Topazes be Entertain'd souldiers in this Garrison.

Souldiers entertained.

Gen^{ll}. Lett^{rs}
from severall
Places read.

The following Generall Letters were now read Viz^t.

From the Generall and Council at Surat dated 25th. April.

From the Deputy Governour and Council at Bombay dated the 13th. and 16th. May last.

From the Deputy Governour and Council of Fort S^t. David dated 31st. August and 2^d. Instant.

Fort S^t.
David Bill for
Pa. 491 : 18.
agreed to be
paid.

The Deputy Governour and Council of Fort S^t. David advise us in their Generall Letter dated 31st. past month that they had drawn a Bill of Exchange on us for P^s. 491 : 18. payable to Somiah, agreed the same be paid.

> THO : PITT.
> WILL : FRASER.
> THO : WRIGHT.
> JOHN MEVERELL.
> TH^{os}. FREDERICK.
> ROB^T. RAWORTH.

Dispatch'd ⅌ Pattamars a Generall Letter to the Deputy Governour and Council of Fort S^t. David dat^d. this [day]

7

Dispatch'd a Generall Letter to the Deputy Governour and Council of Fort S^t. David dated this day [with ten] thousand Pagod^s. under the [charge of Kisnedoss and] Twenty Peons.

10

Received ⅌ Pattamars a Generall Letter from Commodore Brabourne and Council at Anjengo dated 17th. August last with Translate of severall Letters from Mannacuree relating to the Neptunes wrack.

AT A CONSULTATION

Present

TUESDAY
12TH.

THOMAS PITT ESQ^R. PRESIDENT & GOVERN^R.
WILLIAM FRASER.   THOMAS WRIGHT.
JOHN MEVERELL.   THOMAS FREDERICK.
ROBERT RAWORTH.

Comp^s. Cash
for [August]
last] read.
[Sea
Cust]mers
Acco^t. read
for y^e. month
of July, &

Thomas Pitt Esqr. President reads his Account of the R^t. Honble. United Companys Cash for the month of August last Ballance Pagod^s. 13140 : 25 : 5.

M^r. Thomas Wright Sea Customer reads his Sea Custom Account for the month of July last Viz^t.

Custom on Goods Imported & export^d. this month ...	...	...	...	...	Pa. 913 : 17 : 42
Custom on Grain ...	...	...	...	...	444 : 11 : 44
Anchorage	...	...	...	...	55 : 18 : =
Tonnage ...	...	...	...	...	11 : = : 4
					Pag. 1424 : 15 : 6

payes Pa^g.
3148 : 3 : 59
on y^t.

and payes now into the R^t. Honble. United Comp^s. Cash the sume of Three thousand one hundred forty eight Pag^s. three fan. and fifty Nine Cash [as the] Ballance of his former Sea Cus[tom Account] ending ult^o. March last.

————FORT ST. GEORGE, SEPTEMBER 1704————

M^r. Thomas Wright Warehousekeeper reads his Warehouse Account for the month of August last and payes into the R^t. Honble. United Companys Cash the sume of Thirteen thousand four Hundred and Sixty Pag^s. and thirty fanams for Silver and Goods sold out of the Warehouse. *Warehouse. keep^{rs}. Accot. read and payes in Pa. 13460: 30 for Goods sold.*

M^r. John Meverell Paymaster payes into the R^t. Honble. United Companys Cash the sum of sixty Five Pag^s. twenty two fanams, as the Amount of sundrys sold at [Outcry] belonging to Thomas Grandy Deceased. *Ps. 65 : 22 pd, into Cash by Paymast^r. Accot. Grandy [decd.]*

M^r. Thomas Wright payes into the R^t. Honble: United Companys Cash the sume of One Thousand Pagod^s. as part of the Ballance of M^r. Thomas Marshalls Sea Custom Account. *Ps. 1000 pd. Accot. M^r. Marshall's Sea Custom Account.*

M^r. Thomas Frederick Land Customer reads his Land Custom Account for the month of August last. *Land Custom Accot. read.*

Choultrey Custom	...	...	...	...	Pag^s.	148: 21: 20
Rubie broakers ...	...	...	...	...		24: 26: 52
Town Broakers	...	...	...	...		27: 1: 48
Registring Slaves	...	...	...	...		1: 12: =

Pag^s. 201: 25: [40]

and payes into the R^t. Honble. United Companys Cash the sum of six Hundred Pagodas on that Account. *Pagodas 600 pd. in on y^t. Account.*

Generall Letter from Commodore Brabourne &c^a. Council at Anjengo dated the 17th. August last was now read as also Translates of severall Letters from Padre Hieronimo Telles to the Commodore relating to the Neptunes Wreck [with a Letter] from Capt. Lesley. *Anjengo Gen^{ll}. read and severall Papers.*

Ordered that John Lowis, Anthony Farnandus, Manuel Texeres, and Bernardo Ennis be Entertained Souldiers, and John Noble of the Gunroome Crew in this Garrison. *Souldiers and a Gunner [ent^rtain'd]*

We finding it very convenient to keep stores of Salt Provisions not only for the Garrison, but also to supply shipping, and any other unforeseen accident that may happen. Tis therefore agreed that the Steward buys in Three hundred hoggs, to be well fed, and salted up as the Governour from time to time shall direct. *[Hogs] ordered to be [bought].*

There being an order issued out to M^r. Mead Attorney Gen^{ll}. dated the 23^d. August last, for the selling some of Coja Awans Goods to satisfie what he owed for Custom, report of wch. he now makes, and there being due upon the Ballance to Coja Awan Pag^s. 13. 30. 'Tis agreed the same be equally divided between the Secretary and Attorney Generall for their trouble in his business. *[Attorney Gen^{ll}.] delivers in [an acct. what] [seizd] of Coja Awans.*

Agreed this day with Colloway Chittee & Vinkatee Chittee for 2000 Pieces Fine Moorees Long 18 Cov^{ds}. Broad 2½ at Pagod^s. 33 ℗ Corge, and to be sorted by the Comp^{as}. Muster. *Moorees agreed for.*

> THO: PITT.
> WILL: FRASER.
> THO: WRIGHT.
> JOHN MEVERELL.
> THO^s. FREDERICK.
> ROB^T. RAWORTH.

Dispatch'd ℗ Boat a Packett to the Chief and Council of Vizagapatam dated this day. *14*

---FORT ST. GEORGE, SEPTEMBER 1704---

AT A CONSULTATION

Present

THOMAS PITT ESQ^R. PRESIDENT & GOVERNOUR.
WILLIAM FRASER.　　THOMAS WRIGHT.
JOHN MEVERELL.　　THOMAS FREDERICK.
ROBERT RAWORTH.

FRIDAY 15TH.

Generall to y^e. Comp^a. read.　　Generall Letter to the R^t. Honble. United Company dated this day, now read and approved to be sent by a [Danes] ship from Trincombarr.

Petition of the Portuguez presented.　　The Capuchins here of the Portuguez Church being [under] interdictions from the Patriarch and Bishop of S^t. [Thoma] who design to put upon us what Padres they please, [which] may be the worst of consequences, to prevent which ['tis] agreed for the satisfaction of many of our Inhabitants of that Persuation that Padre Laurenso a Capuchin be admitted into Town, to exercise his Function in thei[r Church].

Pa. 1000. pd. in by y^e. Warehousekeeper.　　M^r. Thomas Wright Warehousekeeper payes into the R^t. Honble. United Companys Cash the sume of One Thousand Pagodas on account Goods sold.

Pa. 1000 to be sent to F. St. David.　　Agreed that One Thousand Pag^s. be remitted to Fort S^t. David by Bill of Exchange.

THO : PITT.
WILL : FRASER.
THO : WRIGHT.
JOHN MEVERELL.
THOM^s. FREDERICK.
ROB^r. RAWORTH.

15　　Received ⅌ Patamars a Generall Letter from the Deputy Governour and Council of Fort S^t. David dat^d. 11th. Instant.

16　　Dispatch'd ⅌ Pattamars a Packet to the Governour of Trincombar, wherein Inclosed one for the R^t. Honble. Mannagers for the United Trade to be forwarded by a Ship of theirs there designed in few dayes for Europe.

18　　Received ⅌ Pattamars via Metchlepatam a Generall Letter from S^r. Nicholas Wait & Council at Surat dat^d. 28th. July last.

AT A CONSULTATION

Present

TUESDAY 19TH.

THOMAS PITT ESQ^R. PRESIDENT & GOV^R.
WILLIAM FRASER.　　THOMAS WRIGHT.
JOHN MEVERELL　　THOMAS FREDERICK.
ROBERT RAWORTH.

[Mintmrs.] Acct. read [Pa. 131 : 23:] 40 on y^t. Acco^t. paid. [and Rup^s.] 3279 to y^e. [warehouse] keeper.　　Thomas Pitt Esqr. as Mintmaster reads his Mint Acco^t. for the month of August last, And payes into the R^t. Honble. United Companys Cash the sume of one Hundred Thirty one Pagod^s. twenty three Fanams and forty [cash] for Custom on Gold coined, and payes to the Warehousekeeper Three thousand two hundred seave[nty nine] Rupees as Custom on Silver Coined.

——FORT ST. GEORGE, SEPTEMBER 1704——

M^r. Thomas Wright Sea Customer [reads his] Sea Custom Account for the
month of August [last] Viz^t.

[Sea Custo]
mers Acco^t,
read.

Custom on Goods Imported and exported							
this month	...	...	...	...	Pag^s. 1960:	12:	28
Custom on Grain	...	...	...		74:	11:	—
Anchorage	...	...	...	...	64:	=:	=
Tonnage	...	...	...	...	16:	24:	=

Pag^s. 2,115: 11: 28

M^r. Thomas Wright payes into the R^t. Honble. United Companys Cash for
M^r. Thomas Marshall Late Sea Customer the sum of Nine Hundred thirty six
Pago[das] twelve fanams and seventy four Cash as the Ball[ance] of his Sea
Custom Account ending ult^o. June [last]

Pag^s: 936:
12: 74 p^d.
into Cash
Ball. M^r.
Marsha^{l}ls
Sea Cust.
Account.

The Governour having wrote to Suratt for, so[me oyle] and Paint usefull
here on severall occasions, [as also] some Garden seeds all Amounting to Two
[hundred] and one Rupee 50 P^s. which sum tis ordered [that] the Warhouse-
keeper payes the Governour in Madrass Rupees, and take the aforesaid oyle, [paint
and] seeds for the Companys Account.

Rup^s. 201:
5L p^s. order^d
forP$_a$int &
Gard^{en}
seeds.

The Letter from S^r. Nicholas Wait &c^a. at [Surat] was now read importing
great contests be[tween] S^r. John Gayer &c^a. Council, and S^r. Nicholas &c^a.
[council] copy of our Letter received from them with the [papers] inclosed
we think necessary to be sent to the [Honble.] Mannagers by the conveyance of
the Danes ship but the Packet directed to them we think be[tter] to remain here
to be sent by our own shipp[ing] accordingly 'tis agreed the Packet be forthwith
[despatched] to Trincombar.

Surat Letters
read, ordered
copyes to be
sent ye.
Comp^a.

Agreed that Ten thousand Pagod^s. be sent to Fort S^t. David by Peons
overland, and that the Governour advises them to send their Peons to meet ours
at Connimeer.

[10000 Pag^s.]
to be sent to
F. S^t. David.

Fort S^t. David Generall Letter dated 11th. Instant now read advising of a Bill
of Exchange drawn on this Presidency for Pagod^s. 1327: 23: 3 payable to the
President and Council for the Seperate Affaires of the Old Comp^a. which is agreed
to be paid.

[Fort St.]
David Bill
for [Pag^s.
1327-23-3]
order^d be p^d.

Generall Letter from the Deputy Governour and Council of Fort S^t. David
dated 16th. Instant now read.

[L^r. from
Fort St.
David read].

Generall Letter to the Deputy Governour & Council of Fort S^t. David dated
yesterday now read & approved.

[L^r. to Fort.
S^t. David
read].

THO: PITT.
WILL: FRASER.
THO: WRIGHT.
JOHN MEVERELL.
THO^s. FREDERICK.
ROB^t. RAWORTH.

Dispatch'd ᵱ Pattamar a Generall Letter to the R^t. Honble. Managers for
the United English East India Company Trading to the East Indies.

Dispatch'd ᵱ Pattamarr [two] Packets for Fort S^t. David for the Seperate
and United Affaires [dated the] 18th. and 19th. Instant.

——FORT ST. GEORGE, SEPTEMBER 1704——

AT A CONSULTATION

THURSDAY   *Present*
21ST.

THOMAS PITT ESQR. PRESIDENT & GOVR.
WILLIAM FRASER. THOMAS WRIGHT.
JOHN MEVERELL. THOMAS FREDERICK.
ROBERT RAWORTH.

The Governour and Council of Bencoolen [having late]ly wrote us for a quantity of Copper Cash, and si[l]ver fa]nams, the coining and sending which to them [wee know] to be of great advantage to the Company: 'Tis there[fore] argeed that now being a leisure time in the Mint that the Warehousekeeper buys Ten Candy of [Japan] Copper, and deliver it to the Mintmaster for that [use] as also a Chest of Silver to be coined into Fa[nams].

By Mr. Marshalls laying down the Company['s ser]vice when he went to China, by which the Emp[loy of] the Sea Customer was Vacant, which then [was] [agreed] for the present to be put under the care of Mr. [Wright] for reasons given in our Consultation of the [26th. June] last; But now Mr. Wright having considerable business in the Godowns; 'Tis agreed that Mr. John Meverell succeeds in that Employ, and that Mr. Thomas Frederick [succeeds] him in that [Employ] of Paymaster, and that Mr. Robert Raworth succeeds him in the Employ of Land Customer, and continue Storekeeper till the arrival of Mr. Martin, and that they all Enter on their severall Employes the first of next month and clear their Accounts in their Present Employes.

The Wine Licence expiring the 29th. of this month ordered that on Thursday the 28th. Instant the same be put up to Outcry in the Consultation roome in the Fort before the Governour and Council, and that Notes are fixed on the Gates to give notice of the same.

The Paymaster this day delivering in an Account for building the silk worme Houses and making a Garden for the same Amounting to Three hundred thirty three Pagodas fifteen Fanams. It is again ordered that he puts them up to outcry as mentioned the primo August last, giving notice of the same by putting up Notes on the Gates on the 4th. of October next.

Ordered that Ambon Malajan Topaz be Entertain'd a souldier in this Garrison.

Agreed that one Thousand Pagods. be advanced Mr. John Meverell Paymaster to defray Charges Garrison.

Agreed that Twenty five Pagods. be paid Mannangapau for three months Town Conicoplyes duty ending ultimo July last.

Agreed with Colloway Chittee and Vinkattee Chittee for Moorees ordinary Long 20 Covds. Broad 2½ [No. 1] at Pagods. 19 ꝑ Corge No. 2 : Pags. 18. Two thousand pieces to be sorted by a muster now agreed on [and] seal'd with the Companys and their seal.

THO: PITT.
WILL: FRASER.
THO: WRIGHT.
[*Lacuna*]
THOS. FREDERICK.
ROBt. RAWORTH.

Dispatch'd this evening Kisnados and Twenty [peons] with Pagods. 10,000 for Fort St. David by whom also sent a Generall Letter to the Deputy Governour [and] Council there dated this day.

——*FORT ST. GEORGE, SEPTEMBER 1704*——

Yesterday in the evening we heard that the Portuguez and Moores had 25 had a quarrell wherein was killed a Po[rtuguez] Gentleman Sen[r] John Rebeiro of good fashion and 2 Moores, occasioned chiefly by the Moores Governour going [after a] treacherous manner to his House who they call [the Governaur] of the Portuguez, whom he designed to have mur[dered] or used him barborausly by Imprisonment, he [receiv'd] a slight wound, but upon fireing some Armes [the Moors] Govern[r]. and his People fled, two more of whose people wee hear this day dyed of their wounds, and three or four 'tis said are in [danger] thereof.

About 5 this morning the Governour here received a message from the 26 Governour &c[a]. Portuguez Inhabitants of S[t]. Thoma being come to the Place of our Out Guards who desired admittance and Protection which accordingly was Granted them, and in the evening one of their Chiefest Inhabitants Sen[r]. Matthias Carvallo waited on the Governour, and acquainted him with the whole matter being much as before recited, only that the originall of the quarrell arose from a Moore offering to take a candle from a young Woman as they were walking in procession at their Feast.

————

AT A CONSULTATION

Present

THOMAS PITT ESQ[r]. PRESIDENT & GOVERN[r].
WILLIAM FRASER. THOMAS WRIGHT.
JOHN MEVERELL. THOMAS FREDERICK.
ROBERT RAWORTH.

Tis agreed that the Prisoner brought from Fort S[t]. David for barbarously murthering his Fellow Souldier at Cuddaloor, to be Tryed at a Court Martiall, the method for which to be farther considered of.

The Governour acquaints the Council that according to a Note he received from the Warehousekeeper yesterday he paid Colloway Chittee and Vinkattee Chittee three thousand eight Hundred seventy Nine Pag[s]. being for sundry Callicoes brought into the Warehouse for Account of the United Trade which is now confirmed and approved of.

According to an order of the 21st. of this month the Wine Licence was put up to Farme there being about Four competitors for the same, which fell to Joshua Page['s Lott] he bidding most which was Four Hundred for[ty one] Pagod[s]. ₩ Annum to take a Lease for two yeares we unanimously think one hundred and fifty[Pagodas] too much ₩ Annum, and wish no ill consequence may attend it.

Generall Letter from the Deputy Governour and Council of Fort S[t]. David, dated 24th. Instant now read.

M[r]. Robert Raworth Storekeeper reads his [storekeeper's] Account for the month of August last.

Agreed that one Thousand Pagod[s]. be advan[ced] M[r]. John Meverell Paymaster to defray Charges Garrison.

Ordered that Alphonso Rosairo and Diago [Swares] Topazes be Entertaind Souldiers, and David [Murray] and Humphrey Lencock of the Gunroom [in this] Garrison.

THO: PITT.
WILL: FRASER.
THO: WRIGHT.
JOHN MEVERELL.
THO[s]. FREDERICK.
ROB[r]. RAWORTH.

——FORT ST. GEORGE, OCTOBER 1704——.

29

Received ℔ Pattamar [a Generall Letter from Kittee Nar] rain at Vizagapatam [dated 5th Ins[tant.

OCTOBER
PMO.

Received Two Packets ℔ [Pattamars from the Deputy] Governour and Council of [Fort St. David dated the 27th] past month for the United and Seperate Affairs.

2

Received ℔ Pattamars a Generall Letter from Commodore Brabourne &c⁰. Council at Anjengo dated 9th. September last, advising that the Natives had hall'd ashore ship Neptunes Bottom, but had got little or no Treasure.

3

Received this day ℔ Pattamar a Generall Letter from the Cheif and Council of Vizagapatam dated 11th. September 1704 advising the receipt of the 10,000 Pagod⁰. sent on y⁰. Sᵗ. George Ketch, and their having made a Contract with their Merchants to the Amount of said sum in Longcloth ordinary and Sallampores.

4

Received ℔ Pattamars a General Letter from Mʳ. Thomᵃˢ. Faucet at Metchlepatam dated 20th. September advising of their having miss'd their Port, and arrived at Vizagapatᵐ. from whence came to Metchlepatam, as also a Letter from Kittee Narrain who had likewise mett wᵗʰ. the same fate.

AT A CONSULTATION

Present

THURSDAY
5ᵀᴹ.

THOMAS PITT ESQᴿ. PRESIDENT AND GOVERNOUR.
WILLIAM FRASER.   THOMAS WRIGHT.
JOHN MEVERELL.   THOMAS FREDERICK.
ROBERT RAWORTH.

There being a vacancy in the Council at Fort Sᵗ. David by Mʳ. Empsons refusall to go thither ' Tis agreed that Mʳ. [Richard Farmer be] added as seventh and last [of Council] W[ee haveing had] proposalls from Colloway Chittee and [Vincattee Chittee] for buying of the Broad cloth [received ℔ Martha who] bought that parcell by the Tavestock [part of which is] still upon their hands, we also have had [the] proposealls of Sunca Ramma who refusing to [take the] Cloth Rashes, and Perpetuanoes induced us to agree with the aforementioned Colloway and Vinkattee Chittees a t[wenty] ℔. Cent Profit on the Invoice computing the Pagoda [at] Nine shillings, and are to receive the following [sorts of] Cloth Vizᵗ.

All ordinary Red and Green
All the Aurora
All the Scarlet
All the Cloth Rashes fine and course

All the Perpetuanoes reserving only as much in the Godown as shall be thought necessary for the clothing of souldiers, Presents &cⁿ. a moiety of the whole Amo[unt] thereof to be paid at Three months and the other [moiety] in six months from the time of their receiving it; [what induced] us to so speedy a disposall of the aforesaid [cloth is] partly, what the Honᵇˡᵉ. Managers wrote us by the ['·Mar']tha, from which we inferr a great quantity may be expected by next shipping by reason of the [dearness· of] silver, besides we are not a little apprehensive [that] the Sidney and Loyall Cooke [may chance to bring] hither all their Cloth from China [which would have] much depreciated this should [it lye till] then unsold.

Ordered that the Warehousekeeper [delivers the] aforesaid Cloth, and as soon as done report the Amount to the President and Council.

Our Cash being very low so much that without selling the Silver we are not able to carry on yᵉ. Investments either here or [at]Fort Sᵗ. Davids, and considering that Currant Rupees are already at 360 for Pagˢ. 100 we foresee that if we sell it by Parcells 'twill make Silver very cheap. To prevent which and to be sure of money to carry on the Investments, 'Tis unanimously Agreed that all the Silver now in the Warehouse which is [*lacunæ*] Chests be sold to Colloway Chittee & Vinkattee Chittee at seventeen and one eighth Dollars weight for Ten Pagodas, which is to be delivered them as they pay for the same Vizᵗ. They are to pay on or before the 15ᵗʰ. of this month Twenty five thousand Pagodˢ. on the 15ᵗʰ. of November Twenty five thousand Pagodˢ. on the 15ᵗʰ. of December Twenty five thousand Pagˢ. and on the 25ᵗʰ. January the remainder: Before we agreed on the aforesaid termes we did well and maturely consider this method would be most for the Companys advantage, for tho' we could have sold some few of the Chests att about 16⅝ or 16¾ weighty Dollars for Ten Pagodˢ. yet that would have so adepreciated it, as that the [Company] would have been loosers upon the whole, [besides] upon calculating what we must have paid Interest for money should we have kept it for yᵉ. China Voyage [till May] or June next, which is likewise very [uncertain] without the next ships bring better incouragement then those that came last thence which would have Amounted to more then we could have promysed [our]selves to have Gained by the sale of it at that [time] considering that most of the silver is in [Duccatoons] and French Crownes, which are not so valuable [as] Dollars more especially the former which is [invoic'd] 4¼ Better then standard and in China they [esteem it] but Two ℔ Cent.

Thomas Pitt Esqʳ. President reads his Account [of the] Rᵗ. Honᵇˡᵉ. United Companys Cash for the month of September last Ballance Pagodˢ. 5,934 : 34 : 2

Ponagettee Narso &cᵃ. Tobacco and Beetle ffarmers [pay] into the Rᵗ. Honᵇˡᵉ. United Companys Cash the sume of Five hundred eighty three Pagodas and Twelve [fanams] on that Account.

Mʳ. Thomas Wright Sea Customer payes into the Rᵗ. Honᵇˡᵉ. United Companys Cash the sum of Two [Hundred] and five Pagˢ. for an open Boat received from Metchleptam formerly belonging to the New Company and sold here by Publick Outcry at the Sea Gate.

The following Generall Letters received from severall Places were now read. Vizᵗ.

From Kittee Narrain at Vizagapᵐ. datᵈ. 5ᵗʰ. Septe[mber].
From Comodore Brabourne &cᵃ. at Anjengo 9ᵗʰ. Sept[ember].
From the Cheif & Council at Vizagapᵐ. datᵈ. 11ᵗʰ. Sep[tember].
From the Dep. Governʳ. &cᵃ. at Fort Sᵗ. David 27ᵗʰ. [ditto].
From Mʳ. Faucett at Metchlepatᵐ. 20ᵗʰ. Septem[ber].
From Kittee Narrain dated 19ᵗʰ. September

In the Fort Sᵗ. David Generall now read they advise of their having drawn a Bill upon us for Two thousand five Hundred Pagodˢ. payable to the President and Council here for the Seperate Affairs of the Old Compˢ. Agreed the same be paid, being so much borrowed of their Cash in July last.

Agreed that One Thousand Pagodˢ. be paid Mʳ. Thomas Frederick Paymaster to defray Charges Garrison.

Agreed that we send Two thousand Pagodˢ. to Fort Sᵗ. David by Bill of Exchange.

Agreed that the Paymaster sells the silk worme houses and Garden for the most he can get, according to an order of Consultation on the 21ˢᵗ. past month.

Mʳ. Thomas Wright Sea Customer payes into yᵉ. Rᵗ. Honᵇˡᵉ. United Companys cash the sum of one Thousand Pagˢ. on Account Sea Customs.

Ordered that Andrew Garmarch be Entertained one of the Gunner's Crew in this Garrison and Joan de Rosairo, Lovenso Ferdinando, Peter de Silvia Topazes be Entertain'd souldiers.

————*FORT ST. GEORGE, OCTOBER 1704*————

Ordered that the Accomptant drawes out the Account of the last half year's
salary due to the R'. Honble. United Companys servants here, ending 29th.
Septem'. last.

> Tho : Pitt.
> Will : Fraser.
> Tho : Wright.
> John Meverell.
> Thos. Frederick.
> Rob^r. Raworth.

14th   William Tillard Esq'. the New Com[pany's President at] Metchlepatam advising that he was [at Trevettore] M'. Wright and M'. Raworth went [out to meet]
him, who all arrived here in the evening. He had been upon his Passage twenty
dayes, occasioned by troubles [in the way] which obliged him to come part of it.
by Sea till he was past them : The Governour received him at the Garden when
he fired 15 Great Guns and offered him a room there till those Lodgings in the
Fort which M'. Thomas Marshall had were made ready for him, he also gave him
a Generall Invitation to his Table, and [acquainted] Mons'. Supplie Surgeon and
M'. Eaton Factor who came along with him, that they were both welcome to the
Companys Table.

Padre Landon arrived here this day from Fort S'. [David]

Received a Letter from M'. Thomas Faucet at [Metchlepatam] dated 25th.
September advising that the Yatch and [Fly] were got into Metchlepatam River,
and that they [would] not come up hither this season.

16   Received ℘ Pattamars a Generall Letter from M'. Thomas Faucet at
Metchlepatam dated 3^d. Instant.

18   Received ℘ Pattamars a Generall Letter from the Deputy Governour and
Council of Fort S'. David dated 13th. Instant.

Dispatch'd this evening to Fort S'. David Tw[elve] thousand Pagodas under
the charge of Kisna[das] and Twenty Peons, by whom we also sent a[Packet]
dated this day.

———

AT A CONSULTATION

Thursday
19th.

Present

Thomas Pitt Esq_r. President & Govern^r.
William Fraser.   Thomas Wright.
John Meverell.   Thomas Frederick.
Robert Raworth.

M'. Thomas Wright Warehousekeeper payes into y^e. R'. Honble. United
Companys Cash the sum of Twenty four Thousand five hundred Pagodas on
Account Silver sold out of the Warehouse.

Agreed that Twelve thousand Pagodas be sent to Fort S'. David by Peons
overland of which Two thousand of it is in Bills.

M'. William F_ra_ser Accomptant does now produce an Account of halfe a
yeares Salary due to the R'. Honble. United Companys servants here Amounting
to Pagodas 1,592 : 31 : 2. Agreed the same be paid.

Thomas Pitt Esq'. as Mintmaster reads his Mint Account for the month of
September last, and payes into the R'. Honble. United Companys Cash the sum of
[Thirty Three] Pagodas fourteen fanams and forty Cash for [Custom on Gold]
coined, and payes to the Warehousekeeper [two Rupees] and ten p'.

————*FORT ST. GEORGE, OCTOBER 1704*————

M^r. John Meverell Paymaster reads [his Pay Masters] Account for the month of August last Viz^t.

Charges Garrison	...	...	...	Pag^s.	1,223 :	23
Charges Cattle	...	...	...	...	66 :	35
Silk Wormes	...	...	...	...	3 :	24
Charges Extraordinary	...	...	...		4 :	19
Charges Dyett and allowances	...	...			251 :	10
Stores	...	...	...	...	470 :	27
Charges Generall	...	...	...		337 :	28
Fortification and Repairs		...	...		287 :	18

Pag^s.   2,646 : [4]

M^r. Thomas Frederick Land Customer reads his Land Custom Account for the month of September last w[hich is ap]proved Viz^t.

Choultry Custom	...	...	Pag^s.	127 :	4 :	15[...]
Rubie Broakers	...	...		13 :	29 :	75[...]
Town Broakers	...	...		26 :	15 :	7[...]
Registring Slaves				= :	32 :	[...]

Pag^s.   168 :   9 :   [17]

and payes into the R^t. Honble. United Companys Cash [the] Sūm of Three hundred seventy one Pagodas eleven fanams and 17 Cash, as the Ballance of his Land Custom Account.

M^r. Thomas Wright Sea Customer payes into the Right Honble. United Companys Cash the sum of One Thousand Pagod^s. on Account Seâ Custom.

Agreed that One Thousand Pagodas be advanced to M^r. Thomas Frederick Paymaster to defray Charges Garrison.

Ordered that Anthony De Silvia, Francisco [Rosairo] Lewis Depaigne and Domingo De Rosairo Topazes be Entertained Souldiers in this Garrison.

Agreed that Four thousand Pagodas be p^d. Colloway and Vinkattee Chittees in part for Callicoes brought into the Warehouse.

Ordered that Timothy Allen and George Walker be Entertain'd in the Gun roome Crew of this Garrison.

The following Generall Letters received were now read Viz^t.

From M^r. Faucett at Metchlep^m. dat^d. 25th. Septem^r. 1704.
From   Ditto.   3^d. October
From Fort S^t. David.   13th.   Ditto.

Ordered that the Warehousekeeper sells Lead at Eight Pagodas ℔ Candy.

THO: PITT.
WILL: FRASER.
THO: WRIGHT,
JOHN MEVERELL.
THO^s. FREDERICK.
ROB^r. RAWORTH

[Received ℔] Pattamar a Generall Letter from Commodore [Brabourn] &c^a. 24th Council at Anjengo dated 30th. past month [inclosing] copyes of severall Letters to and from Captai[n Lesly who] was in the Company's [Munchua at Mannacurree] near the Neptune's [wreck giving] great [ho pes] of recovering the Treasure, part of the bottom of the ship not being in above Nine foot of water.

Dispatch'd ℔ Pattamars the following Generall Letter all dated 23^d.

-------*FORT ST. GEORGE, OCTOBER 1704*-------

AT A CONSULTATION

Present

THOMAS PITT ESQ^R. PRESIDENT & GOVERNOUR.
WILLIAM FRASER.   THOMAS WRIGHT.
JOHN MEVERELL.   THOMAS FREDERICK.
ROBERT RAWORTH.

TUESDAY 24TH.

The following Generall Letters sent to the undermentioned Places dated this day, were all now read and approved and ordered to be Copyed out fair Viz^t.

> To Kittee Narrain at Metchlepatam.
> To M^r. Thomas Faucet at Ditto.
> To the Chief and Council at Vizagapatam.
> To the United Council in Bengall.
> To the Deputy Govern^r. &c^a. at Fort S^t. David.
> To the Commodore &c^a. Council at Anjengo.
> To S^r. Nicholas Wait &c^a. Council at Surat.

To the Deputy Govern^r. &c^a. Council at Bombay. Agreed that Eighteen Hundred Ninety one Pagodas thirty one fanams be paid [out of cash for] Callicoes. brought into the Warehouse by Com[raupau Chittee.]

THO. PITT.
THO^S. WRIGHT.
WILL. FRASER.
JOHN MEVERELL.
THO^S. FREDERICK.
ROB^T. RAWORTH.

27TH.

Dispatch'd ℔ Pattamars the following Generall Lres all dated the 24th Instant Viz^t. ;

> To Kittee Narrain at Metchlepatam.
> To M^r. Thomas Faucet at Ditto.
> To the Chief and Council at Vizagapatam.
> To the United Council in Bengall.
> To the Deputy Govern^r. &c^a. Council at Fort S^t. David.
> To the Commodore &c^a. Council at Anjengo.
> To S^r. Nicholas Wait &c^a. Council at Surat.
> To the Deputy Governour &c^a. Council at Bombay.

31ST

Rec^d. ℔ Pattamars a Generall Letter from the Deputy Governour and Council of Fort S^t. David dated 24th. Ins^t. advising the safe arrivall of the 12,000 Pagod^s. sent them.

NOVEMBER 2ND

Received this day a Packet from S^r. John Gayer &^a. Council at Surat dated the 13th. September with Copyes of theirs of the 24th. August sent Via Bengall, advising that the Surat ship the Pyrates tooke on that Coast last year was lost near Syndee the Pyrats having all left her at Don Maskareen, and Madagascar, where at the latter they gave her to the Laskars who endeavoured to carry her to Surat but lost her as beforementioned, they likewise advise us that the Dutch had seiz'd Three Moors Mocho ships of great value, where was also several Pilgrims of considerable Quality, all which they positively refused to deliver till they had permitted the [Di]rectore and all their Companys servants to withdraw from Surat, or deliver them up their security Papers and Nineteen Lack of Rupees for the Dammages [they] had suffered by them in their Trade. S^r. John [Gayer &c^a.] at Surat were all under strict Guards, and [the Men] of Warr at the Rivers mouth, but had no power [to assist] them.

————*FORT ST. GEORGE, NOVEMBER 1704*————

Present

THOMAS PITT ESQ⁣ᴿ. PRESIDENT & GOVERNOUR.
WILLIAM FRASER.   THOMAS WRIGHT.
JOHN MEVERELL.   THOMAS FREDERICK.
ROBERT RAWORTH.

Ponagettee Narso &cᵃ. Tobacco and Beetle ffarmers pays into the Rᵗ, Honᵇˡᵉ. United Companys Cash the sum of [five] hundred eighty three Pagodas twelve fanams on that Account.

The President acquaints the Council that he paid on the 2ᵈ. Instant the sum of Four thousand four hundred eighty eight Pagodas to Colloway and Venkattee Chittees for Calicoes brought into the Warehouse by them as advised by the Warehousekeepers Note.

Thomas Pitt Esqʳ. President reads his Accounts of the Rᵗ. Honᵇˡᵉ. United Companys Cash for the Month of October last Ballance Pagodas 7643 : 3 : 4.

Thomas Pitt Esqʳ. as Mintmaster reads his Mint Accᵗ. for the month of October last, and payes into the Rᵗ. Honᵇˡᵉ. United Companys Cash the sum of sixty three Pagˢ. as the Ballance for Custom on Gold coin'd in the Mint.

Mʳ. Thomas Wright Warehousekeeper reads his Warehouse Accounts for the month of September last.

Mʳ. Thomas Wright Sea Customer Reads his Sea Custom Accounts for the month of September last Vizᵗ.

Custom on Goods Imported & Exported	...	Pa.	1,190 :	4 :	74	
Custom on Grain	... ...	„	371 :	25 :	32	
Anchorage	... ...	„	77 :	18 :	=	
Tonnage	... ...	„	22 :	8 :		

Pa. 1661 : 20 : 26

and payes into the Rᵗ. Honᵇˡᵉ. United Companys Cash the sum of One Thousand Pagodas on Account Sea Customs.

Agreed that One Thousand Pagodas be advanced to Mʳ. Thomas Frederick Paymaster to defray Charges Garrison.

The following Generall Letters received were all now read Vizᵗ.

From the Deputy Governʳ. &cᵃ. at Fort Sᵗ. David dated 24ᵗʰ. of October 1704.

From Sʳ. John Gayer &cᵃ. Council at Surat 13ᵗʰ. Sepʳ. 17[04]:

From Dittos datᵈ. 13ᵗʰ. Sepʳ. 1704 relating to Ship Prosper[ous.]

From Dittos dated 24ᵗʰ. August 1704 Copy.

Copy of a Perwanna from Hassat Han to yᵉ. Govʳ. of Surat.

Ordered that Salvadore De Mount be Entertained one of the Gunners Crew, and that Jos : Mentoro Me Rodrigues Abre Mendez, Domingo de Costa, Francisco de [Meneza] be Entertained Souldiers in this Garrison.

The Musketts that were sent out on the [Martha being] of a different bore to those formerly sent, 'Tis [ordered] that the Warehousekeeper delivers the Gunner [. . .] Candy Lead to make shott for them.

'Tis Agreed that Antonio De Miha a Chinese [who] kill'd his fellow Souldier at Fort Sᵗ. David be [tried] by a Court Martiall at the Companys

m

———*FORT.ST. GEORGE,· NOVEMBER 1704*———

Garden [House] on Wednesday next the 15th. Instant, and that M^r. Matthew Mead Attorney Generall do in the mean time draw up a charge against him, and get the same Translated into the Portuguez Language.

> THO: PITT.
> WILL : FRASER.
> THO : WRIGHT.
> JOHN MEVERELL.
> THO^s. FREDERICK.
> ROB^t. RAWORTH.

15 · · This being the day appointed as ℔ order of Consultation [of] the 10th, Instant, to hold a Court Martiall for Trying Antonio De Miha, 'Tis deferred, M^r. Mead the Attorney Generall being ill.

16 Dispatch'd ℔ Pattamars the following Generall Letters dated the 14th. Instant Viz^t.

> To M^r. Faucet at Metchlepatam.
> To the Chief and Council of Vizagapatam.
> To the President and Council for the Seperate Affaires in Bengall.
> To the United Council in Bengall.
> To the Deputy Governour &c^a. at Fort S^t. David.

18 Dispatch'd ℔ Pattamar the following Generall Letters dated this day.

> To M^r. Faucet and Kittee Narrain at Metchlepatam.
> To the Chief and Council at Vizagapatam. .

22 Received ℔ Pattamars a Generall Letter from M^r. Thomas Faucet at Metchlepatam dated 10th. Instant advising the great apprehensions of troubles all Europeans were in there by reason of those at Surat, which they fear will effect them, the Dutch in particular making great preparations for their defence, who are advised their Cheif at Golcondah is seiz'd, and 25,000 Rupees demanded of them.

This day M^r. Matthew Mead Senior. Merchant in the R^t. Honble. United Companys Service departed this Life.

23 Yesterday in the evening we saw a smack to the northward which came to an Anchor about seven, a Clock and this morning the Master came ashore and acquaint'd us it was the Rising Sun Smack [come] from Bengall belonging to the R^t. Honble. [United] Company Loaden with Petre &c^a. by her [were receiv'd] the following Packets.

> From the United Council in Bengall [dated 19th August 1704].
> From Ditto dated 4th. November.
> From the United Council in Bengall dat^d. 6th Nov[ember 1704]
> From Ditto dated [*lucuna*].
> From Messrs. Bugden and Eyre dated 9th. Novem^r. [1704].

This day arrived the Huglyana Ketch Charles [Hopkins] Master by whom we received a Generall Letter from Governour and Council of York Fort dated 24 [th August] 1704.

———FORT ST. GEORGE, NOVEMBER 1704———

AT A CONSULTATION

Present

THOMAS PITT ESQᴿ. PRESIDENT & GOVERNOUR.
WILLIAM FRASER, THOMAS WRIGHT.
JOHN MEVERELL. THOMAS FREDERICK.
ROBERT RAWORTH.

Generall Letter from the Deputy Governour & Council of Fort Sᵗ. David dated 11ᵗʰ. Instant was now read advising of their having drawn a Bill of Exchange on us for Four hundred Pagodˢ. payable to Mʳ. Richard Hunt, which Bill being now presented, Agreed the same be payd.

Agreed that One Thousand Pagodas be paid Mʳ. Thomas Frederick Paymaster to defray Charges Garrison.

Mʳ. John Meverell late Paymaster reads his Acco[unt] for September last, Vizᵗ.

Charges Garrison	...	...	...	P. 1288 : 8
Charges Cattle	...	...	...	39 : 17
Charges Dyett and allowances		...		247 : 21
Stores	...	...	...	79 : 4
Fort Sᵗ. David ...	...	...	...	1 : 18
Charges Generall	...	...	...	366 : 32
Charges Extraordinary		...	...	2 : [23 . . .]
Fortification & repairs		...	...	195 : [22 . . .]

Pagˢ. 2221 : 1 [. . .]

and payes into the Rᵗ. Honᵇˡᵉ. United Companys Cash the sum of One Thousand and seven Pagodas and three fanams as the Ballance of his Paymasters Account.

Mʳ. Thomas Frederick Paymaster reads his paymasters Account for the month of October last Vizᵗ.

Charges Garrison	...	...	...	...	Pagˢ. 1216 : 19 :
Charges Cattle	...	...	...	...	40 : 8 :
Charges Dyett and allowances		...	...		244 : 33 :
Stores	...	...	...	...	52 : — :
Charges Generall	...	...	...		351 : 35 :
Charges Extraordinary	...	...	...		18 : 5 :
Fort Sᵗ. David ...	...	...	...		8 : 23 :
Fortification and repairs		...	...		72 : 22 :

Pagˢ. 2005 : 1 :

Peter de Pomere &cᵃ. Arrack Farmers payes into the Rᵗ. Honᵇˡᵉ. United Companys Cash the sum of seven Hundred Pagodas on that Account.

Mʳ. Thomas Wright Warehousekeeper payes into the Rᵗ. Honᵇˡᵉ. United Companys Cash the sum of Seven Thousand one hundred Ninety eight Pagodˢ. eighteen fanams, being the full Amount of Broadcloth sold at the Sea Gate to Colloway Chittee, which money has been some time due, but he having not sold the Cloth delayd the payment thereof till this time.

Agreed that Eight Thousand Pagodas be paid to Colloway and Vinkattee Chittees in part for Callicoes [brought] into the Warehouse by them.

Agreed that Fifteen thousand Pagodas [be sent by] Peons overland to Fort Sᵗ. David.

Mʳ. Thomas Wright Warehousekeeper payes into the Rᵗ. Honᵇˡᵉ. United Companys Cash the sum of [ten] thousand pagodas in part of silver sold Colloway & Vinkattee Chittee.

m-1

————*FORT ST. GEORGE, NOVEMBER 1704*————

Huglyana Ketch arriveing from the West [Coast] [this] day by whom we received a Generall Letter fr[om the] Governour and Council of York Fort dated [24th. August] advising the great number of Bills drawn [by them] by Ship Queen were on Account of the Unit[ed Trade] the consideration of which is deferred to our [next meeting].

Ordered that Robert Atkinson be Entertain[d one of the Gunners Crew in this Garrison.

THO: PITT.
WILL: FRASER.
THO: WRIGHT.
JOHN MEVERELL.
THOˢ. FREDERICK.
ROBᵀ. RAWORTH.

AT A CONSULTATION

Present

THOMAS PITT ESQ². PRESIDENT & GOVERNOUR.
WILLIAM FRASER.   THOMAS WRIGHT.
JOHN MEVERELL.   THOMAS FREDERICK.
ROBERT RAWORTH.

FRIDAY
24ᵀᴴ.

The Rising Sun Smack Thomas Harris Master [arrived] yesterday in this road from Bengall Laden with Salt Petre, ordered that the Warehousekeeper do unload the same with all expedition in order to her proceeding to ship Neptunes wreck.

Ship Dutchess Capᵗ. Hugh Raymond Commander arriving in this road this day from Bengall who brougᵗ. us a Generall Letter from the United Council in Bengall dated 9th. March 1703/4 which was now read. Ordered that the Warehousekeeper do unload all the Goods & Stores belonging to the United Company on board said ship, except the Salt Petre which is to be continued on board as part of her Kentilage.

Mʳ. Matthew Mead Senior Merchant in the Rᵗ. Honᵇˡᵉ. United Companys service dyed on the 22ᵈ. Instant, and no Will to be found, ordered that Mʳ. Thomas Frederick and Mʳ. Robert Raworth do take an Inventory of the said Mʳ. Meads Estate and report the same to this Board.

Ordered that the Huglyana Ketch be forthwith dispatch'd to Fort Sᵗ. David in order to goe into that River to be sheathed and cleaned, and that the Deputy Governour and Council there, have directions to do it with all expedition, that so she may returne Laden with the Companys Bales hither, and that the Fifteen thousand Pagodˢ. agree[d] yesterday to be sent thither overland be now Laden on Her.

Ordered that the Warehousekeeper sends on the Huglyana Ketch good store of Packing stuff of all sorts to Fort Sᵗ. David and that the Storekeeper sends thither a new Beam, and puts on board her Nails &cˢ. that will be wanting for her Sheathing.

This day Colloway and Vinkattee Chittees complained to us against Sunca Rama, That he bought up Cloth in the Country for which they had given out money for the Company, besides that he very much inhanced the Price, to which if we did not put a speedy stop, they could goe no further on in the Investment: Sunca Rama was sent for who confest good part of what was charged against him,

——FORT ST. GEORGE, NOVEMBER 1704——

for which he was repremanded by the President and told that tho'. the Company allow'd to all their Inhabitants freedome of Trade, yet [it was] to be in such a manner as not to be any wayes [to their] prejudice.

> THO: PITT.
> WILL: FRASER.
> THO: WRIGHT.
> JOHN MEVERELL.
> THOS. FREDERICK.
> ROBT. RAWORTH.

AT A CONSULTATION

Present

THOMAS PITT ESQR. GOVERNR. AND PRESIDENT.
WILLIAM FRASER.　THOMAS WRIGHT.
JOHN MEVERELL.　THOMAS FREDERICK.
ROBERT RAWORTH.

MONDAY 27TH.

Generall Letter from Mr. Thomas Faucet at Metchlepatam dated the 16th. Instant now read.

Yatch and Fly formerly belonging to the New Compa. at Metchlepatam arriving to day in this road from thence, ordered that the Storekeeper unloads them wth. all expedition.

Agreed that one Thousand Pagodas be paid Mr. Thomas Frederick Paymaster to defray Charges Garrison.

Thomas Harris presented a Petition to be reinstated in his former Employ as Ensign, The consideration of which is deferred till we see a thorow reformation in him.

It being agreed in a former Consultation that Serjt. Dixon and Serjeant Hugonin should goe to Comand the Souldiers that we are now about sending to the Neptunes wreck and considering that the giving ym. the Character of Ensigns Pro hac Vice would strengthen their Command over the souldiers. 'Tis therefore agreed that they have that Character in their commission which is to be signed by the Governour and that ye. Paymaster advances Two months Pay to them as also to all the Men.

Agreed that Mr. Thomas Woolmer Surgeon be Entertain'd at eight Pagodas ⅌ mensem for this expedition, and that he gives a Bond of 500 Pags. penalty that he leaves not the service when he comes to the wreck without leave from Mr. Brabourne or he that Commands in Chief there.

Ordered that the Paymaster advances three months Pay to all the Masters, Sailers and Laskars on board the Vessells now bound to the Neptunes wreck.

This day wee tooke into consideration [the payment] of the West Coast Bills which amounted [to, Interest] and all, near Forty thousand Pagods. & consid[ering] that if we pay them at this present we must [stand] still with the Investment, so 'Tis resolved [that· wee] deferr them if possible till the arrivall of the [China Ships,] and in the mean time those that are not contented with their Bills ; 'Tis Agreed that they have Bonds given them signed by the President and Council for the payment of the same at Interest at eight per cent. 28TH

> THO: PITT.
> WILL: FRASER.
> THO: WRIGHT.
> JOHN MEVERELL.
> THOS. FREDERICK.
> ROBT. RAWORTH.

FORT ST. GEORGE, NOVEMBER 1704

This day the Governour received a Letter from M[r]. Adams Chief at Callicutt advising him that Ketch Tibby Ca[p]t. George Weoley Commander was [brought] in there by a small French ship that sa[iled] lately from Pollicherry having met the said [Ketch off] Ceilone.

AT A CONSULTATION

Present

THOMAS PITT ESQ[a]. GOVERN[r], & PRESIDENT.
WILLIAM FRASER.   THOMAS WRIGHT.
JOHN MEVERELL.   THOMAS FREDERICK.
ROBERT RAWORTH.

There being a cause in the Court of Admiralty before M[r]. Thomas Marshall layd down the Judges Employ, relating to the case of M[r]. Hall to which M[r]. Empson and M[r]. Carey in this Place has some claime to a part that is in Bengall; about which M[r]. Warr this day Regis[r]. to that Court produced a Letter from M[r]. Sheldon and M[r]. Curgenven; the consideration of which is deferred to an other opportunity.

M[r]. Richard Farmer importuning us to be Entertained as last of Council at Fort S[t]. David, and was admitted as by a former Consultation, since which he has been very troublesome in Importuning the Governour by Letters for Land Customer & Scavenger at Cuddaloor in which Employ M[r]. Games was fixed on the first settlement of the Council there, and being on some Account or other jealouse that he should not obtain it, we received from him this day a Generall Letter mennaceing what he [would do if] he had not those employes, for which reason [as well as] Judging that he has no particular right to [the]m, ' tis] resolved that M[r]. Games continue in them [and that] M[r]. Farmer has such an Employ as is at this [time va] cant.

We inferring from the Letters from Anjengo [that they] are bare of money, and not knowing but they may [want] to subsist the Neptunes Sailers, as also the men [we now] send. ' Tis agreed that One Thousand Pagod[s]. be sen[t on] the Rising Sun, and Five hundred Pagod[s]. on the Maddapollam Yatch.

Generall Letters to the Deputy Governour & Council of Fort S[t]. David, and to the Commodore &c[a]. Council [of] Anjengo, both dated this day, now read and approved.

Ordered that John Tea one of the Gunners Crew at his request be discharged from farther Service in [this Garri] son.

M[r]. Thomas Wright Warehousekeeper pay[s] into the R[t]. Hon[ble]. United Companys Cash the [sum of] Three thousand Pagod[s]. on Account Silver [and Goods] sold.

M[r]. Thomas Wright Late Sea Customer re[ads his] Sea Custom Account Currant for the month[s of October] and November last, and payes into the R[t]. Hon[ble]. United Companys Cash the sum of Eleven [Hundred] and five Pagodas ten fanams and sixty Cash as the Ballance of that Account.

M[r]. Robert Raworth Storekeeper reads his [Accounts] for the months of September and October last.

—————FORT ST. GEORGE NOVEMBER 1704————— .

M.ʳ Robert Raworth Land Customer reads his Land Custom Account for the month of October last, Viz.ᵗ ·

Choultry Custom	...	...	...	..	Pag.ˢ 111:	30: 45
Rubie Broakers	...	...	...	...	39:	—: 36
Town Broakers	...	...	...	...	2:	2: 24
Registring Slaves	...	...	...	...	2:	8: —

Pag.ˢ 155: 5: 25

Agreed that Four Hundred Pagodas be advanced to Paulo &c.ᵃ Washers towards curing the R.ᵗ Hon.ᵇˡᵉ United Companys Cloth, and that the Warehouse-keeper delivers them out of the Godowns six Garce of Rice.

Generall Lett.ʳ from Mess.ʳˢ Griffith and Bugden at Atcheen dated 6ᵗʰ August last now read.

THO. PITT.
WILL. FRASER.
THO. WRIGHT.
JOHN MEVERELL.
THO.ˢ FREDERICK.
ROB.ᵀ RAWORTH.

Ketch Boneadventure Samuel Butcher Master arrived in this Road from Bengall.

[DECE]
MBER
1ˢᵗ.
2

Huglyana Ketch Charles Hopkins Master sailed out of this road for Fort St. David by whom sent a Gen.ˡˡ Letter to the Deputy Governour and Council, there dated 30ᵗʰ. past month.

This day arrived a Packett from the Commodore &c.ᵃ Council at Anjengo dated 9ᵗʰ. past month advising the arrivall there of Two Separate Stock [ships] the Horsham and Anne M.ʳ Walter Combes [Supra] Cargoe bound to Surat. and departed Engl[and 9ᵗʰ April,] the said Letter advices of the arrivall at [Goa] of two Portuguez ships from Europe.

AT A CONSULTATION

Present

THOMAS PITT ESQ.ᴿ GOVERN.ᴿ AND PRESID.ᵀ
WILLIAM FRASER. THOMAS WRIGHT.
JOHN MEVERELL. THOMAS FREDERICK.
ROBERT RAWORTH.

SATURDAY
2ᵈ.

The following Letters &c.ˢ received and sent now read, Viz.ᵗ :—

From Commodore Brabourne &c.ᵃ Council at Anjengo dated [9ᵗʰ November] 1704

From Dep.ᵗʸ Govern.ʳ &c.ᵃ Council at Bombay 13ᵗʰ Septem[ber] 1704.
Sailling orders to y.ᵉ Master [of the] Rising Sun Smack.
Sailing orders to y.ᵉ Master of y.ᵉ Maddap.ᵐ Yatch
Governours Commissions to y.ᵉ two Ensigns bound to y.ᵉ Neptune's wreck.
Govern.ʳˢ Letter to y.ᵉ Chief Minister in Mangomaus [Country].
Generall Lett.ʳ to y.ᵉ Govern.ʳ of Columbo or Gallee.

Agreed that one Thousand Pagodas be advanced to M.ʳ Thomas Frederick Paymaster towards build[ing]the Black Town Wall and Works.

THO. PITT.
WILL. FRASER.
THO. WRIGHT.
JOHN MEVERELL.
THO.ˢ FREDERICK.
ROB.ᵀ RAWERTH.

------FORT ST. GEORGE, DECEMBER 1704------

4. Yesterday evening the Masters of the severall Vessells bound to the Neptunes wreck had their Dispatches given them when immediately the souldiers ordered upon them embarkt and the vessells sailed in the night.

6. Ship Dorothy Richard Rose Master arrived in this Road from Vizagapatam and Metchlepatam by whom received the following Letters Viz'.

2 Generalls from the Cheif and Council of Vizagapatam dated 20th. and 27th. November with Copy of the Diary and Consultations from Septemr. 4th to November 19th.

From Mr. Faucett and Narrain dated 29th. November Inclosing Bill of Loading for 59 Bales Chay Goods and 3 Sallampores loaded on this Vessell.

From Mr. Faucet dated 28th and 29th. November last.

From Kittee Narrain dated 3d. Instant.

AT A CONSULTATION

[THURS.]
DAY 7TH.

Present

THOMAS PITT ESQ^R. PRESIDENT & GOVERNOUR.
WILLIAM FRASER.   THOMAS WRIGHT.
JOHN MEVERELL.   THOMAS FREDERICK.
ROBERT RAWORTH.

Agreed that the Bill of Exchange drawn by the Deputy Governour and Council of Fort St. David dated 31st. August last for Four hundred ninety one Pagod'. eighteen fanams be now paid unto Somiah, the payment of which having been deferred so long by reason of a dispute between him and Seraupa &c'. Joint Stock Merchants.

The Rice brought up now by the Dutchess being much dammaged by wormes; 'Tis Ordered that the [Warehouse] keeper sells it all at the Banksall for the [most he can] gett.

The Governour does now acquaint the Council [that] he had detected three Black Fellowes of runing of [cloth] that came out of the Country to cheat the Company of their Customs, who were now before us, one of them being charg'd with Betteelas found in his House which had no [chop of] the Custom House, to which he answered that the Company's chop being only redd earth wash't out, & [produced] a choultry Note, for a parcell of Betteelas brought in last year for Mr. Marshall, of which these [now taken] he sayes were those he turned out. The other two black fellowes being charged with hyding Long cloth fine in a House little distance from the Town, [and Fareing] it into small peices of 14 Cov^ds. or thereabouts [to wear] in as Turbants and Girdles, of which they made frivolous excuses saying they intended to have brought it [to] the Custom House, and that there was only two pieces taken by a Servant to cover him from the Rain, [they were] all sent Prisoners to the Choultry till further [inquiry] could be made.

Coja Timore presented a Petition representing that there was some Goods amongst Coja Awans [that] properly belonged to Coja Usuph, which suffered much by lying, and if they were not speedily taken [care of would] be eaten up by the white Ants; Agreed that the [Governour] and any one of the Council examine what [alledg'd in] the Petition and do what fitting therein.

The Measurers presented a Petition as Entered after this Consultation insisting upon a greater allowance for executing that office then what we told them they should have formerly in Consultation without which they are not able to subsist the People they were forced to keep for that service, The consideration of which is deferred to our next meeting.

Joshua Page presenting a Petition complaining of frauds put upon him in the Wine License by Henry Hunt, orderd they attend next Councill day.

———FORT ST. GEORGE, DECEMBER 1704———

Thomas Pitt Esq⁰. President reads his Account of the Rᵗ. Honᵇˡᵉ. United Companys Cash for the month of Novemʳ. last Ballance Pagodˢ. 1,292 : 17 : 3.

The following Letters received were now read, Vizᵗ.
2 Letters from Cheif and Council Vizagapᵐ. datᵈ. 20ᵗʰ. & 27ᵗʰ. Novʳ. 1704.
From Mʳ. Faucet dated 28ᵗʰ. and 29ᵗʰ. November.
From Mʳ. Faucet and Narrain datᵈ. 29ᵗʰ. Ditto.
From Kittee Narrain 3ᵈ. December.

Ordered that James Aveline at his request be discharged from farther service in this Garrison as also Peter Dewell.

Messʳˢ. Frederick and Raworth do now deliver in an Inventory of Mʳ. Matthew Mead Decᵈ. Estate Ordered yᵗ. they sell the same at Publick Outcry at the Sea Gate.

Ordered that the Warehousekeeper Embales Brown Longcloth and Sallampores as they come in clean.

Mʳ. John Meverell late Paymaster, reads his Account of the Black Town Wall and Works from Aprill to the ultimo September last, and pays into the Right Honᵇˡᵉ. United Companys Cash One Hundred twenty [eight pagodas] Nineteen fanams and seventy one Cash [being the] ballance of that Account.

> Tho: Pitt.
> Will : Fraser.
> Tho : Wright.
> John Meverell.
> Thoˢ. Frederick.
> Robᵀ. Raworth.

Ship Speedwell arrived from Vizagapatam.

Received ⅌ Pattamars a Generall Letter from the Deputy Governour and Council of Fort Sᵗ. David datᵈ. 8ᵗʰ. [Instant.]

12

At a Consultation

Present

Thomas Pitt Esqᴿ. Governˢ. and Presidᵀ.
William Fraser.   Thomas Wright.
John Meverell.   Thomas Frederick.
Robert Raworth.

Thursday 14ᵀᴴ.

William Tillard Esqʳ. delivers in a Paper as Entered after this Consultation the purport of which being to ask our advice relateing to some Affairs of the New Company, upon which we call'd him in, and desired him to descend to particulars, and wee should be ready to serve the new Company to the utmost of our Power in all respects, so first he desired that we would supply him with what money we could out of the United Companys Cash for Account of the New Company, that so he might in some measure appease the clamours of their Merchᵗˢ. at Metchlepatam to whom they were considerably Indebted, unto which he was answered that we had no orders from the Managers of the United Trade to supply either of the Seperate Interest of the Old or New Company out of their Cash, besides we are at this time very much streighten'd for money to provide Cargoes for the speedy dispatch of the ships belonging to the United Trade, Mʳ. Tillards next request that since we could not supply him with money, to advise him what answᵉre he shoᵈ. make the Merchants, who he heard was coming up hither, as also whether we would advise him to remain here or goe for England by the first ship, unto which was replyed we could think of no

n

————FORT ST. GEORGE, DECEMBER 1704————

other answere to be given to the Merchants then that they must have Patience till the New Company sent out money or give orders therein, and that we thought it not only the Companys Interest, but his own, as also the Merchants that he goe for England by the first ship, carrying with him all necessary Bookes and Papers, whereby to give the Company a full and intire Account of their Debt at Metchlepatam, which we think the most effectuall way to bring it under their consideration for the speedy payment thereof, and further that he leaves Copys of all Bookes and Papers here to be sent [to] the Comp⁰. by the next yeares Ships.

The Governour produces a Gentue Letter which was found on Monday last by Ensign Poirier at the Sea Gate sealed up and directed to the Governour which being Translated we find the purport of it, is complaints of frauds committed by the Storekeepers, Rent [all Gen]erall and Scavengers Conicoplyes, about which [there] was a Gentue Letter near a month since dropt [in the] Companys Garden importing much the same [but neither] of them descending to particulars so as to detect frauds therein mentioned: 'Tis Agreed that the [follow]ing Paper be published by setting [it] up in all [Languages] at the Sea Gates.

That Whereas there has been lately Gentue [Letters] dropt at the Sea Gate and Companys Garden [directed] to the Governour the purport of which is complaints of frauds committed by the Storekeeper, Rentall [Generall] and Scavengers Conicoplyes, but not descending to particulars we are not able to detect the same. Therefore this is to certifie that if that Person or Persons who wrote the Letters will appear before the Governour and Councill and prove what therein alledged against the [Conicoplys] he or they shall not only have Fifty Pagodas reward but likewise be protected by the Government as also employed for their future Incouragement.

There having been further inquiry into the business of Moota, a Black Fellow who was suspected of running of Betteelas, 'tis believ'd they are as he alledges a parcel turn'd out by Mr. Marshall, and for not haveing the Choultry chop upon them 'twas answer'd 'twas alwaies done with red earth which came out in Washing, so to prevent frauds for the future of this nature, 'Tis order'd that the Land Customer chops all Goods at the Choultry with such marking stuff as is us'd at the Godown, which comes not out with washing, and is hereby agreed, for the foregoing reasons, Moota be releas'd.

Ponnagettee Narso &c⁰., Tobacco and Beetle Farmers, pays into the Right Honble. United Company's Cash the Sum of Five Hundred Eighty three. Pagodas Twelve fanams on that Account.

Thomas Pitt.
William Fraser.
Thomas Wright.
John Meverell.
Thomas Frederick.
Robert Raworth.

To the Honble. Thomas Pitt Esqr.
  President of the Coast of
    Choromandell & Governour of
      Fort St. George &c^a. Council

Sheweth

The Humble Petition of Pencoola Kisna Bowchee that your Hon^r. &c^ss. Petitioners has been Measurers of Paddy to the Right Honble. Company many years, in which Office they alwaies behav'd themselves honestly, Your Hon^r. &c^ss. Petitioners had for each Garse measuring formerly from the Buyers four fanams per Garse, and from the Sellers 2 fanams per Garce, which they had allow'd them all along in Hon^r. Higginson's time, and some years in your Hon^r.

&c². time, and now only allow'd forty Cash per Garce at present, and if Paddy. fall cheaper, as by all likelyhood it will considering the Season &cⁿ., they will perhaps only pay twenty Cash per Garce, by which means your Honʳ. &cᵃˢ. Petitioners are allready allmost ruin'd by running in debt to pay their Servants to the Number 34, which is merely impossible they can assist themselves or familys long, and in a little time will be reduced to such want, they shall not have wherewithall to sustain Nature without your benign &cᵃ. prevent the ensuing calamity, which can only be prevented by allowing them what they formerly had per Garce from Buyer and Seller as is aforesaid, May it please your Honʳ. &cᵃ. for each Pagodas worth they had one Measure, and now but eight part of a measure for each Pagoda, all which is very hard to your Petitioners, they putting their sole Repose in your Honʳ. &cᵃˢ. goodness.

Your Petitioners humbly intreat that you may take the premises into your serious consideration and grant them their request as formerly and as in duty bound shall ever pray &cᵃ.

To the Honᴮᴸᴱ. Thomas Pitt Esqᴿ.
  President &cᵃ. Council for the United
    Affairs of Yᴱ. Rᵀ. Honᴮᴸᴱ. English
      East India Compᵃ. on the Coast of Choromandell.

Hnᴮ ᴸᴱ. Sᵗ. &cᵃ.

Having occasion for your advice hope you'l excuse the trouble of these lines from one who is destitute of Council occasioned by the mortality of all those whom the Honᵇˡᵉ. East India Company sent out to consult together about the Mannagement of their Affairs; I do therefore draw up for your perusall a short breviary of occurrences which have happend since the beginning of our troubles with the Merchants at Metchlepatam, which will give your Honʳ. &cᵃ. an insight into the occasion of their continuance to this day Vizᵗ.

President John Pitt Esqʳ. and myself, the rest of the Council being dead, sent Home and consigned to the Directores in London on ships Stretham & Rising Sun in February and April 1702 for Account of the Honᵇˡᵉ. East India Company Sundry Goods and Merchandize amounting to upwards of 253,000 Pagˢ. part of which sum is already [payd] at Metchlepatam, and we were in hopes of paying off the rest at the arrivall of the first ship from England, but it was our misfortune to be disappointed by the loss of ship Norris the 2ᵈ. of August following, however the Merchants to whom the Ballance of said money was owing, considering that such a Loss was not by the carelessness of [or could] be prevented by any one ashore, they were very well contented to stay till the shipping came out the next year (in case we did not recover any thing from the wreck, in finding which we were also disappointed not only of the Treasure which came in the No[rris] but in the Loss of our President John Pitt Esqʳ. above mentioned who dyed in May 1703 at Duram [Parr, so] many disappointments following one the other [made] the Merchants very uneasy and troublesome [to me] the survivor; but yet I did a little mollifie [their] uneasy tempers by telling them we expected [the] Hallifax every day from China, which according[ly] did arrive in July following; out of which I [took] out all the Gold and what Merchandize would sell at Metchlepatam satisfying the Merchants in part with said Gold and Merchandize which made them contented to st[ay till] the arrivall of the next Europe ships from the [Directores.]

The latter end of December following we received the newes of the Tavestock arrived at this Place [for] [account] of the United Trade, but there being no money come out by Her to pay the Merchants, I did again [satisfie their]

------FORT ST. GEORGE, DECEMBER 1704------

uneasiness by telling them that the Directors [could] have yet no Account of the loss of the Norris by which ship they had sent out money, but when the next ships came be sure we shall have money sent out by them.

In August last we received news of the arrivall of yᵉ. Martha from England for Account of the United Company and at the same time I received a Letter from the Honourable Directors wherein was no mention made of any money sent out by them to pay the Merchants, which made them very hott in their Demands on me to know the reason of the Companys not sending out wherewithall to satisfye their Debts, I could not have told what answere to make them, had we not at the same time received the displeasing newes of the Neptunes runing a shoar on Cape Comoreen, when I told them that the Directors might very probably send out money by said Ship Neptune, but she miscarrying and the Letters with Her, I could have no Account of the truth thereof, and withall told them 'twould be necessary for me to goe to Fort Sᵗ. George not only to enquire whether any money belonging to our Company came in said ship, but in case there was none sent out by Her, then I could request your Honour &cᵃ. Council to spare me some money out of that wᶜʰ. belong'd to the United Company; the Merchants were notwithstanding this answere still very uneasy and dissatisfyed, some of them being for my staying at Metchlepatam till they received what was due to them; but afterwards they all considered better of the matter, and consented to my coming hither where I have been now arrived almost two months, still in expectation to hear some good news from the Neptunes wreck [but] your Honour &cᵃ. having yet received no good account thereof from Anjengo concerning the wreck and the time of the Europe ships departure from hence drawing very nigh; I do now put in this my request to Your Honour &cᵃ. Council for your advice to me in my circumstances.

First what answere I shall give to the Merchants in respect to the money which is come for [Account of] the United Company, and if it do's not suit with [yʳ.] Judgements or occasions to part with any money then [pray] give me your advice how I shall further Act [in yᵉ.] Affaires of my Employers, your opinions herein may be very serviceable to the Honᵇˡᵉ. Company and will be gratefully acknowledged by my forwardness [in what]soever may be serviceable to the United Company [or] yourselves being

	Honᵇˡᵉ. Sʳ. &cᵃ.
Fort Sᴿ. George	Yoʳ. most Humᵇˡᵉ. [Servant]
13ᵗʰ December 1704.	William Tillard.

15ᵀᴴ   This evening the Governour received advice [that Doud] Cawn was arrived at Conjeeveron, and that he [design'd for] Sᵗ. Thoma.

16ᵀᴴ   Received ℞ Pattamar a Generall Letter from Commodore Brabourne &cᵃ. Council at Anjengo dated 17ᵗʰ [November] advising that the Natives had severall times attempted to dive for the Neptunes wreck but were beaten off by Capᵗ. Lesly in the Nunchu; Inclosed in said Letter was copy of a Letter from Mʳ. Adams &cᵃ. at Calicut dated 8ᵗʰ. November advising the arrivall of four French ships of considerable force at Punella half a League to the Southward of Tellicherry. We also received this day a Letter from the Governʳ. and Council of Negapatam advising also the arrivall of the French Ships, and inclosed copys of Lettʳˢ. from their severall Chiefs on that Coast, who farther advise that the French had engaged near Mangalore two Portuguez Frigats of 26 and 24 Guns [whom] they tooke, one they burnt, and the other sent with [the] Prisoners to Goa, they had likewise taken a [ship] in the Latitude of Bombay belonging to the [Brok]er there, they give out they are bound for Pollicherry but for a certainty is yet unknown.

———FORT ST. GEORGE, DECEMBER 1704———

Rec^d. ℔ Pattamar a Generall Letter from the Deputy Governour and Council of Fort S^t. David dated [*lacuna*]. [also in T.O. copy.]

This day arrived Kittee Narrain from Metchlepat^m. with whom came 17 Merchants from thence (being above twenty) to demand of M^r. William Tillard what money was due to them from the New Company.

Dispatch'd this morning a Packet to Mr. Faucett at Metchlepatam inclosing 17 copyes of the Letters we rec^d. which advised of the arrivall of the French ships, ordering him to dispatch the same immediately to Vizagapatam and from thence to Bengall with all expedition.

Boneadventure Ketch Samuel Bowcher Master sailed for the Coast of Mallabar 17 by whom sent a Generall Letter to Commodore Brabourne &c^a. Council at Anjengo.

———

At a Consultation

Present

Monday 18th.

Thomas Pitt Esqr. Govern^r. and President.
William Fraser.   Thomas Wright.
John Meverell.   Thomas Frederick.
Robert Raworth.

By Consultation November the 10th. 'twas appointed on the 15th. following Antonio de Mayo should be [brought] upon his Tryall for stabbing his fellow souldier & accordingly M^r. Mead was ordered to draw up his Ind[ictment,] who presently after fell sick and dyed, so that wee having no Person here so proper for that employ, and there being five Wittnesses that lyes at Charge. 'Tis agreed that they are all taken into service in the military till an opportunity presents for Trying the aforesaid Persons, and then to return to Fort S^t. David.

Kittee Narrain delivers in an Invoice of the [chey Goods] &c^a. bought by him at Metchlepatam with his [account] Currant and Charges: ordered that the Accomptant [examin] aforesaid Invoice and Accounts and report [the same] next Consultation.

The President and Council mett this day [at the] Warehouse to view the Metchlepatam Goods, which came out tollerably well, and much cheaper then formerly, they also made the head muster for Fine Long cloth and Sallampores and ordinary Brown Longcloth, and Agreed that the Musters N°. 2 and 3 should be made by the sorters at the Warehouse as they sort the Cloth, and produced to this Board for their approbation.

This day Colloway and Vinkattee Chittee's were before us to agree the prizes of the Fine Long cloth and Sallampores for which we thought they ask'd extravagant, [for] which reason we deferred concluding with them till the sorters compared it with Cloth imbaled in the Godown of the same sorts.

On the 22^d. March 170⅔ the Governour and Council in Consultation unanimously agreed that Nichola Manuche's Lease for his House and Garden should be renewed for twenty one yeares all which relating to that matter is as Entered after this present Consultation, but just as the Lease was drawing the Governour received a Letter from a Padre at Negapatam full of strange Invectives against Senr. Manuch which was produced to the

——FORT ST. GEORGE, DECEMBER 1704——

Council, wherein there was many expressions which filled them with jealousys. that he. was not true to the Companys Interest, for which reason 'twas. agreed the Lease should be stopt till inquiry be made into the truth of the Letter, and the Character of the Person that writt it, who upon very good inform— ation we found that the Padre was an infamous and scandalous fellow, and that the [sor^{ce}] of this Letter arose from Manuches Detecting his attempting to committ debaucherys in his Family, besides the Padres of this Place and other Portuguez Inhabitants of good reputation gives the aforesaid Padre a very ill. Character, and having from the time the Lease was stopt to this present strictly inspected the Action of Senr. Manuch we find no reason to change our former good opinion of him. 'Tis therefore unanimously agreed that the Secretary Drawes him out a Lease upon the Termes first intended.

The following Generall Letters received were all now read.

From Fort S^t. David dated (*Lacuna*) [*also in T'.O. copy.*]
From M^r. Faucett dated 6th. December
From Anjengo dated 17th. November
From Callicut to Anjengo dat^d. 8th. Ditto
From Negapatam 20th. December N.S.

M^r. John Meverell Sea Customer reads his Sea Custom Account for the month of October last Viz^t.

Custom on Goods imported & exported this moth.	P.	367 : 31 : 28
Custom on Grain		8 : 9 : 86
Anchorage		17 : — —
	Pag^s.	393 : 4 : 64

Thomas Wright Warehousekeeper reads his Warehouse account for the month of October and November last and payes into the R^t. Honble. United Companys Cash the sume of Nineteen thousand six hundred sixty one Pagodas in part of silver sold out of the Warehouse.

Agreed that Nineteen Thousand six hundred sixty one Pagodas be paid out of Cash to Colloway & Vinkattee Chittees in part of Callicoes brought into the R^t. Honble. United Companys Warehouse as ℔ the Warehousekeepers Note.

Tho. Pitt.
Will. Fraser.
Tho. Wright.
John Meverell.
[*Lacuna*]
Rob^r. Raworth.

Thursday
22^d.

AT A CONSULTATION

Present

Thomas Pitt Esqr. Govern^r. and President.
William Fraser.   Thomas Wright.
John Meverell.   Thomas Frederick.
Robert Raworth.

M^r. Thomas Wright Warehousekeeper payes into the R^t. Honble. United Companys Cash the sume of Five thousand Pagodas on Account Silver sold.

—————*FORT ST. GEORGE, DECEMBER 1704*—————

The following General Letters sent were now read.
To the Deputy Govern^r. and Council of Fort S^t. David.
To Governour Comans &c^a. Council at Negapatam both dated this day.
Generall Letter from the United Council in Bengall dated 22^d. past month
now read.

The Accomptant do's now report that he has perused the Invoice and Papers relating to the Investment [made] at Metchlepatam by Kittee Narrain who finds no [Error] therein.

The Kings Buxee this day making a Vissett to the Governour, who has showed himself friendly to the Companys Interest on all occasions, to preserve which Tis agreed that we make him the following Present.

    1 Piece of Scarlet
    1 Ditto of Aurora
    1 Ditto ordinary Red
    1 Ditto Green and to his servants 10 y^{ds}. Aurora

The Sea Customer reports that some Gunnys and other Goods freighted on Ship Dutchess from Bengall are dammaged, and that M^r. Affleck to whom they were consigned, desires a surveigh may be made thereof and such reasonable allowances made as we think fit. Resolved that the Dammaged Goods before mentioned be surveyed by Four indifferent Persons, M^r. Edward Fleetwood M^r. George Heron for the Company, and the Two others to be chosen by M^r. Affleck, and that the Sea Customer [reports] what they determine, so as the Company may be [advised] what they suffer thereby, and if they find it reasonable to deduct it out of the ships Freight.

The Warehousekeeper reports that as he is delivering out to the Merchants the Broad Cloth, he finds that some of it is a little damag'd by moth &c^a. in so much that they refuse to take it without some allowance. Resolved that the Warehousekeeper, Messrs. Fraser and Meverell survey the same and adjust the damage with the Merchants, which when done the Warehousekeeper to report it to this Board.

Order'd that the Warehousekeeper Loads on board Ship Dutchess her charterparty proportion of Redwood.

Agreed that One thousand Pagodas be advanced to Mr. Thomas Frederick, Paymaster, to defray Charges Garrison.

Agreed that Four Hundred Pagodas be advanc'd to Mr. Robert Raworth, Storekeeper, to buy brimstone to refine for Gunpowder.

PARAGRAPH TO FORT S$_T$. GEORGE CONSULTATION THE 22D MARCH 1702-3 VIZ^T. :

Mr. Nichola Manuch his Lease being expir'd for a house and Garden he has in the Suburbs of the Black Town, which was planted by him, 'tis order'd that the Lease for the same be renew'd for twenty one years to come, he paying for the same sixty Pagodas.

It being the Generall Opinion of all that the aforesaid Mr. Nichola Manuch is very poor, and in consideration of his readiness to serve the Company on all occasions, 'Tis agreed that upon his payment of the sixty Pagodas before mentioned, it be return'd him as a gratuity for his good Services.

Ship Sedwick, Captain Rawlings, Commander, arriv'd in this Road from 22^d. Bengall, by whom receiv'd a Generall Letter from the United Councill there dated 22d November last.

Dispatch'd per Pattamarrs Generall Letters to the Governour and Councill 23^d. of Negapatam, and to the Deputy Governour & Councill of Fort St. David, both dated yesterday.

————FORT ST. GEORGE, DECEMBER 1704————

27ᵗʰ.   The following Order was Sign'd by the Governour and Councill:

Yessama Naigues son still remaining at Trivlecane, I am advis'd 'tis for the Company's Interest that wee take some Notice of him by making him a Present, for that he is in a considerable Post and Governs a Country from whence comes many Goods for this Town, and thô those I advise with think the following present too small, I am for adding no more, and desire your Opinions upon it.

     1 Piece Scarlet.
     1 Dᵒ. Ordinary Red.
     1 Dᵒ. Green.
     2 Sword Blades.
     1 Small looking Glass.

                         THOMAS PITT.
                         WILLIAM FRASER.
                         THOMAS WRIGHT.
                         JOHN MEVERELL.
                         THOMAS FREDERICK.
                         ROBERT RAWORTH.

INDEX

A

Abdee Sallam, 18.
Abraham Malay, 25.
Acheen, 12, 13.
Adams (Capt.), 51, 94, 100.
Addison, Gulston, 2, 37, 53, 58.
Affleck (Mr.), 2, 3, 6, 103.
Ainsworth, George, 55.
Allebux, 16.
Allemadutt, 29.
Allemud, 18.
Allefaunde, 18.
Allen, Timothy, 87.
Alphonso Rosairo, 83.
Ambon Malajan, 82.
Amoy, 43.
Angelus, T. Michael, 7.
Anjengo, 18, 19, 38, 63, 66, 70, 74, 76, 79, 84, 85, 87, 88, 94, 95, 100—102.
Anne, 95.
Anthony De Silva, 87.
Anthony Secare, 70.
Antonio de Mayo, 101.
Antonio de Miha, 89, 90.
Antonio de Rosera [Rosaro], 59, 70.
Antonio Johanna, 44.
Antonio Fereiro, 10.
Arrackan [Arracan], 4, 38, 47.
Assed Cawn, 15.
Atcheen, 2, 13, 14, 29—32, 35, 43, 56, 95.
Atkinson, Robert, 92.
Audney, Nicholas, 41.
Augustine de Rozira, 38.
Aveline, James, 97.

B

Banksall, 96.
Barrow, Nathaniel, 5.
Bastion Carvalla, 38.
Bastion Lewall, 44.
Batavia [Battavia], 10, 23, 57, 59, 75.
Beard (Pres^t.), 35, 37.
Bedford, 50
Bencoolen, 38, 42, 54, 58, 59, 82.
Bengal [Bengall], 1, 2, 5—7, 11, 12, 16, *passim*.
Bentall, 53.
Benyon (Mr.), 42.
Bernard de Mount, 66.
Board (Pres^t.), 18.
Bombay, 25, 61, 77, 78, 88, 95, 100.
Bomborupang [*Bombarupum*], 29, 76.
Bone, 38, 47.
Boneadventure, 95, 101.
Boomipollam, 67.
Boon, Charles, 7.
Bowcher, Samuel, 47, 101.
Boyce, Peter, 12.
Brabourne, Commodore, 63, 66, 70, 74, 76, 78, 79, 84, 85, 87, 93, 95, 100, 101.

Brewster (Mr.), 10, 12, 15, 43.
Bugden, Charles, 12–14, 26, 28, 29, 31, 32, 90, 95.
Bulkley, Edward, 2, 14, 42.
Bulkley, Ralph, 27, 29.
Burrish (Capt.), 57.
Butcher, Samuel, 37, 95.

C

Callicutt [Calicut], 94, 100, 102.
Cape Commareen, 63, 100.
Carey (Mr.), 94.
Carvallo, Matthias, 83.
Canterbury, 4, 5, 10, 11, 14, 17.
Canton, 42, 43, 52.
Cawn Bahaudear, 15.
Ceilone, 1, 94.
Chambers Frigat, 5, 14, 23, 25, 87.
Charles, 47.
Charlton, 77.
China, 3, 10, 23, 43, 48, 51–54.
Chinandee Chittee, 46, 55.
Chineapatam [Chinapatam], 15, 22, 26.
Christian Quintus, 54.
Coda Bux, 42.
Coja Auganure, 47.
Coja Awan [Cojati Awannah], 24, 27–29, 42, 50, 51, 54, 57, 60, 61, 74, 79, 96.
Coja Issup [Issop, Usuph], 27, 51, 54, 58, 60, 61, 74, 96.
Coja Mark, 16.
Coja Michael, 43.
Coja Paulo, 27, 60.
Coja Phanuse, 61.
Coja Sattore [Satoor], 35, 56.
Coja Timore, 24, 26-28, 50, 54, 57, 58, 60, 61, 74, 96.
Cojah Woanes, 29.
Cojee Gregoree [Gregorey, Gregoria], 14, 15, 24, 54.
Cujee Tanerre, 76.
Colchester, 2, 3, 5, 6, 11, 24, 28, 39, 41, 60.
Colloway Chittee, 55, 56, 64, 66, 69, 75, 79, 82—85, 87, 89, 91, 92, 101, 102.
Columbo, 95.
Combes, Walter, 95.
Commerce, 23, 29, 38, 41.
Comraupau Chittee, 88.
Coniers (Mr.), 12.
Conjeeveron, 100.
Coningsby (Mr.) 42.
Connimeer, 67.
Cornwall (Cap.), 70.
Covelong, 41.
Cowes (Mr.), 63.
Cuddaloor, 77, 94.
Curgenven (Mr.), 94.

D

Daniel (Mr.), 10, 43.

o

Dansburgh, 57.
Davenport, Henry, 53, 74.
Daud [Doud, Dowed] Cawn, 3, 4, 15, 26, 27, 33, 50, 100.
Delton (Mr.), 32.
Destiny, 41, 77.
Dewell, Peter, 97.
Diago Swares, 83.
Dinna Ketch, 25, 56, 57.
Dixon, William, 5, 93.
Dolben (Mr.), 5, 14, 23, 43, 48, 52, 53.
Dolphin, 26.
Domingo de Costa, 89.
Domingo de Rosairo, 87.
Domingo de Roz, 10.
Domingo Leam, 4.
Don Maskareen, 88.
Dorothy, 36, 77, 96.
Dundee Madrass, 25.
Duramparr, 99.
Dutchess, 2, 92, 96, 103.

E

Eaton (Mr.), 86.
Edwards (Capt.), 77.
Ellis, Francis, 17, 19, 25.
Emas, John, 21.
Emoy, 10, 23.
Empson, Matthew, 75, 84, 94.
Endeavour, 57, 78.
England, 2, 5, 57, 62, 95, 99, 100.
Ennis, Bernardo, 79.
Ephram de Nevers, 65.
Etterick, Anthony, 63.
Europe, 95.
Eyre (Mr.), 90.
Eyton (Mrs.), 53.
Eyton, Nathaniel, 53.

F

Farmer, Richard, 84, 94.
Farnandus, Anthony, 79.
Faucett (Mr.), 4, 70, 71-73, 84-86, 88, 90, 93, 96, 97, 101, 102.
Fets, Michael, 26.
Fleetwood, Edward, 103.
Flint (Capt.), 10, 11, 87, 43.
Fly, 66, 86, 93.
Fontenay, Monseiur de, 5.
Ford (Capt.), 77.
Forowke, Randall, 66.
Fort St. David, 2-8, *passim*.
Fort St. George, 1-8, *passim*.
Fort William, 28.
France, 32, 56.
Francis, 41.
Francisco, 27.
Francisco Cordoza, 75.
Francisco de Costa, 77.
Francisco de Meneza, 89.
Francisco De Saa, 75.
Francisco Rosairo, 87.
Fraser, William, 1-8, *passim*.
Frederick (Mr.), 14.
Fremen, Stephen, 5, 28, 29, 34.
Frewen (Mr.), 5.
Friend (Mr.), 42.

G

Gabriel de Costa, 12.
Gallee, 95.
Games (Mr.), 94.
Ganjam, 11, 27.
Ganjees, 11.
Garmarch, Andrew, 85.
Gatt, Andrew, 43.
Gayer, John, 77, 81, 88, 89.
Goa, 38, 95, 100.
Golcondah, 22, 90.
Gombroone, 47, 52.
Goodman, Samuel, 62, 76.
Gostlin (Capt.), 77.
Gralvis, 45, 47.
Greenhaugh (Capt.), 17.
Greyhound, 37.
Griffith (Mr.), 13, 14, 31, 32, 95.
Grimes, Richard, 10, 11.
Grupa [Gruapah], 10, 23, 47.

H

Hall (Mr.), 51, 70, 94.
Hancock (Capt.), 29.
Happyness, 38, 47.
Harnett (Mr.), 76.
Harris (Ensign), 9, 55, 92, 93.
Harrison, Jeremiah, 26.
Harrison, Richard, 5.
Hart (Capt.), 57, 78.
Hassat Han, 89.
Haveningham, Villers, 5.
Heaton, Samuel, 59, 75.
Heirusalem, 16, 76.
Henning (Mr.), 23.
Heron (Capt.), 17, 103.
Hieronimo Telles, 79.
Higginson (Honr.), 98.
Hiller, Joseph, 4, 21, 45.
Holcombe, Simon, 71.
Holland, 59.
Holycross (Mr.), 11.
Hopkins, Charles, 36, 54, 90, 95.
Horsham, 95.
Hugonin (Serjeant), 75, 93.
Hugley, 18.
Hughlyana Ketch, 36, 37, 44, 49, 54, 90, 92, 95.
Humphrey, 47, 59.
Hunt, Henry, 96.
Hunt, Richard, 8, 91.
Hunt, Robert, 9, 26, 29.

I

Ignatius (Senhr.), 18, 33.
Isaac Malay, 25.

Jakernacolo, 2.
Jennings, William, 42, 58.
Joan de Rosairo, 85.
Johanna, 55, 56.
Jones, Edward, 49.
Josiah, 38.

K

Ketch, 49.
Kingsford (Capt.), 5, 6, 10.

Kisnados [Kisnedoss], 67, 76, 78, 82, 86.
Kittee Narrain, 50, 67, 68, 71, 72, 84, 85, 88, 90, 96, 97, 101, 108.

L

Landon (Padre), 17, 86.
Latchee Prasaude, 70.
Latchms, 29.
Laulchad (Noquedah), 47.
Laulusaunder, 4.
Laurenso (Padre), 80.
Lecroy, Thomas, 9.
Legg (Capt.), 37, 38, 49, 52.
Lencock, Humphrey, 83.
Lesley (Capt.), 63, 66, 79, 87, 100.
Lewis Depaigne, 87.
Lisbon, 57.
Lister, Joseph, 53, 58.
Littleton, Edward, 18.
Lockyer, Charles, 88.
Lovenso Ferdinando, 85.
Lowis, John, 79.
Loyall Cooke, 62, 68, 84.
Lyde, James, 5.

M

Madagascar, 88.
Maddapollam, 4, 47, 94, 95.
Madapollam, 5, 70, 72.
Madrass [Madrassapatam], 15, 20.
Mahomudde, 25, 77.
Mahomud Hussain, 70, 77.
Mahomud Tyre, 25.
Malacca, 5, 23, 32, 52, 53, 76.
Malborough, 10, 23.
Mallabar, 101.
Mangalore, 100.
Manilha, 18, 54, 61.
Mannacurra [Mannacure], 63, 78, 87.
Manuch (Sr.), 101, 102.
Manuel Caldera, 77.
Mannangapah, 17, 44, 82.
Mare (Capt.), 18.
Marshall, Thomas, 1 – 8, *passim.*
Martha, 57, 62, 63, 68, 69, 74, 76, 84, 89, 100.
Martin, Matthew, 18, 82.
Mary, 59, 70.
Master, Edward, 41.
Matthews, Thomas, 39.
Maverell, John, 1–8, *passim.*
Mead, Matthew, 57, 58, 61, 79, 90, 92, 97, 101.
Mergee, 18.
Merino, Antony, 51.
Metchlepatam [Mechlepatam], 1, 4—6, 8, 9, 12, 16, 22, 23, 34—37, 41, 43—45, 48, 57, 61, 62, 66, 69—73, 76, 80, 84—86, 88, 90, 93, 96, 97, 99, 101, 103.
Michael (Padre), 6, 7.
Miguel, Anjo, 65.
Minister, Landon, 5.
Minter (Capt.), 10, 23.
Mirusmaun, 22.
Mooseeraude, 18.

Moota, 98.
Mootombee Moodelaree, 17—20.
Morrice, William, 38.
Moyers (Capt.), 11.
Munchua, 87.
Murray, David, 83.
Musell Taunapa, 20.

N

Naggapau, 35.
Nalla Mutty, 46.
Narrain, 39, 59.
Narasapore, 16.
Negapatam, 29, 45, 60, 73, 100-103.
Neptune, 57, 62, 63, 66, 68, 75, 79, 84, 87, 94—96, 100.
Nevell (Mr.) 25.
Nichola Manuch, 101, 103.
Nicholas (Sr.), 81.
Nina Chittee, 51.
Noble, John, 79.
Norris, 99, 100.
Nunchu, 100.

P

Page, Joshua, 83, 96.
Parker, Joseph, 25.
Parren Gregoria, 50.
Pasquall De Costa, 74.
Pasquall De Grace [Grasse], 44, 51.
Patamar [Pottamar], 1, 2, 4, 6, 8, 11, 16, 35, 37, 38, 43, 46—48, 61, 62, 70, 73, 76, 78, 80, 81, 84, 86, 87, 90, 97, 100, 101, 103.
Paula Doulat, 35.
Paul De Silva, 70.
Paupiah, 45, 74.
Pearle, 76.
Peddaway Duppa, 35.
Pegu Nulla Sanady, 56.
Pegue, 29, 33, 35, 39, 77.
Pembrooke Frigat, 43.
Pencoola Kisna Bowchee, 98.
Peria Virapa, 20.
Perring (Capt.), 38, 47.
Persia, 24, 27, 37, 38, 47, 48, 52, 53, 73, 76.
Persiawaeke, 67.
Peter de Pomera, 19—21, 23, 47, 60, 91.
Peter de Silva, 85.
Peterson, Adreon, 55.
Philips, John, 24, 51.
Pianacaut, 26.
Pitt, Thomas, 1-8, *passim.*
Plumb, Thomas, 26.
Poirier (Ensign), 98.
Pollicondore, 23, 36, 53.
Pollicat, 4, 45, 73.
Ponagette Narso, 10, 23, 35, 37, 46, 55, 64, 77, 85, 89, 98.
Pondicherry [Policherry], 4—7, 10, 17, 56, 94, 100.
Pool, John, 25.
Portugall, 57.
President, 17.
Prince Charles, 6, 37.
Prosperous, 89.
Pullemullee, 18.

Q

Queddah, 17.
Queen, 37, 38, 42, 48-54, 92.
Queen Anne, 2, 9, 10, 14, 27, 32.

R

Ramdos, 65.
Rawdon, Edward, 18.
Rawlings, Richard, 29, 47, 103.
Raworth, Robert, 2, 19, 25.
Rawon Rautoon, 35.
Rayes, Mark, 51.
Raymond, Hugh, 92.
Rebeiro, John, 83.
Reid, Alexander, 5.
Restoration, 38, 47.
Ridley (Capt.), 57.
Rising Sun [Rising Sun], 59, 60, 70, 90, 92, 94, 95, 99.
Roberts (M .), 7.
Rodregues, Antonio, 55.
Rose (Capt.), 36, 96.

S

St. Cruize [Cruce, Cruz], 18, 47, 54.
St George, 57, 76.
St Joan, 43.
St Joan de Canterbury, 54.
St. Johan, 35.
St. Thoma, 22, 24, 26—29, 33, 39, 50, 57, 62, 74, 80, 83, 100.
Salvadore De Mount, 89.
Sambelam Island, 5.
Sammon, Thomas, 17.
Samuel, 11,
Sands (Capt.), 38, 47.
Scattergood (Mr.), 76.
Scipio, 57.
Scarlet, John, 5.
Sebastian Rebeira, 44.
Sedgwick [Sedwick], 47, 103.
Sedgwick (Capt.), 29.
Seermary, 47.
Serapan [Seraupau], 4, 59, 74, 96.
Shaw, George, 39, 40.
Sheik Abdasalam, 15.
Sheldon (Mr.), 94.
Sidney, 53, 84.
Slyland, Johannes, 45.
Slyland, Monheer, 73.
Soames (Mr.), 51.
Somiah, 78.
South, Thomas, 14, 37.
Spain, 32.
Speedwell, 97.
Stock, Joseph, 55.
Stone (Mr.), 7.
Stretham [Strutham], 10, 12, 13, 15, 16, 23, 37, 41, 43, 99.
Sultan Demollet Aulum, 31.
Sumarteen, 29, 42.
Sunca Rama, 50, 65, 84, 92.
Supplie, (Monsr.), 86.
Surat [Suratt], 5, 6, 18, 19, 31, 38, 39, 43, 47, 61, 62, 73, 77, 80, 81, 88, 89, 95.
Surat Merchant, 29.
Syndee, 59, 88.

T

Tandermine, John, 55.
Tandore, 67.
Tanjore, 50.
Tavestock [Tavistock], 1—3, 7, 8, 10, 11, 17, 18, 22, 39, 40, 42, 99.
Tea, John, 94.
Tellicherry, 100.
Texeres, Manuel, 79.
Tibby ketch, 56, 94.
Tillard (Mr.), 1, 5, 6, 8, 9, 22, 23, 34, 35, 37, 43, 44, 48, 53, 57, 61, 62, 71—73, 76, 86, 97, 101.
Tompson, George, 8.
Trevettore, 86.
Trincombar, 10, 37, 45, 50, 54, 58, 60, 76, 80, 81.
Trivlecane, 104.
Tutecoreen, 76.
Twisden (Capt.), 76.
Tyher Cawn, 18.

U

Ulumbane, 10.

V

Venture Desire, 77.
Vincattee Puttee, 56.
Vincattee Yerwallapa Madua, 56.
Vinkattee Chittee, 55, 64, 66, 69, 75, 79, 82—85, 87, 89, 91, 92, 101, 102.
Vizagapatam, 2, 3, 12, 16, 35, 36, 39, 41, 43, 46, 59, 67, 71, 76, 79, 84, 85, 88, 90, 96, 97.
Vizagapatam Merchant, 27, 35, 43.
Vizapore, 22.

W

Wait, Nicholas, 61, 62, 73, 80, 81, 88.
Walker, George, 87.
Wallaca [Woolacca] Chittee, 46, 55.
Wallis, Peter, 39.
Warr, William, 3, 42, 61, 94.
Warren (Mr.), 51.
Watts, Richard, 39, 40.
Weld, Matthew, 5.
Weld, William, 57, 76.
Weoley (Capt.), 59, 94.
West Coast, 5, 38—40, 44, 48, 49, 53, 54, 92.
Wheeler, Charles, 39.
Whistler, Henry, 54.
White (M .), 51.
Woolmer, Thomas, 93.
Wright (Capt.), 47, 59.
Wright, Thomas, 1-8, passim.
Wyburgh (Capt.), 59, 60, 70.

Y

Yatch, 66, 86, 93.
Yegmore, 67.
Yessama Naique, 104.
York Fort, 37, 38, 40, 57, 90, 92.

Z

Zypher Cawn, 18.